THE TVA

An Approach to the Development of a Region

THE TVA

An Approach to the Development of a Region

By GORDON R. CLAPP

 THE UNIVERSITY OF CHICAGO PRESS

CHARLES R. WALGREEN FOUNDATION LECTURES

Library of Congress Catalog Number: 55–5119
THE UNIVERSITY OF CHICAGO PRESS, CHICAGO 37
Cambridge University Press, London, N.W. 1, England
The University of Toronto Press, Toronto 5, Canada

Foreword

Six months have passed since I left the Tennessee Valley. As May 18, 1954, approached—the anniversary of the TVA Act of 1933 and coincidentally the end of my term as a member and chairman of the board of directors—this note to employees appeared on the bulletin boards throughout the offices, construction jobs, power plants, and miscellaneous places scattered through the Valley where TVA work gets done:

> This is TVA's Twenty-first Birthday. It is also the end of my twenty-one years with TVA.
>
> Goodbye and good luck. My deepest thanks to a great organization for the rewarding experience I have shared with all of you.
>
> I know TVA under the leadership of its experienced and devoted Board will continue to do its best to maintain and improve the high standard of public service these twenty-one years have established.
>
> In the months and years ahead don't let little minds or the greedy intimidate or enchant you or divert you from your service to the public interest.

This was my last official communication with the twenty-two thousand men and women of the Authority whose work and intelligent devotion to a great public purpose furnish the substance of this book. This book is dedicated to them, to the many state and local officials, and to the tens of thousands of citizens of the Tennessee Valley and elsewhere who have found a workable way of co-operating for a greater public good.

The problem of our day—as it has been every day in the history of mankind and always will be—is to find such workable ways in order

v

to discover the key to a *faith* in ourselves and in more and more of our fellow-men. In that way, and in that way only, can we extend and strengthen the boundaries of a secure community within which our talents for unfrustrated living can expand and work the miracles of which human talents are capable.

The word "faith" is abstract, but the opportunities to express the idea by our daily actions and decisions are unmistakably real. Faith in one's self and in others is more than an attitude. It is a necessary complement to the will to act—to do something or to refrain from doing. Its counterpart may be fear. Certainly one need not argue that we have found workable ways to discover and nourish our fears. We can mobilize every man-hour, every nut and bolt, into a gigantic effort of destruction to support our faith in our more limited community when a fear of strangers, ambitious in their insecurity, pervades our lives. But, without fear, the prosecution of works of faith becomes a spasmodic part-time job.

Because we have so little faith, we drift along until we feel compelled to resort to direct force and power to exact submission from others. Our personal problem is to find and use the inner wellsprings of propulsion that produce a graceful and effective life of thought and decision lifted above the cheap and degrading influence of fear.

In discussing a matter of belief, for such is our subject, generalizations beyond our actual experience can have little validity in the scientific sense. In the realm of man's faith and beliefs the data of human aspirations and conduct are largely unmeasurable by the devices of the laboratory. But we can build hypotheses from our own experiences. From the testimony of the experience of others we can strengthen our willingness to run the risk of trying them. For that reason I agreed to give the Walgreen Foundation Lectures on which this book is based and to state the facts about one great adventure in faith and works.

The scene is a great river coursing from its tributaries high in the mountains of Virginia and the Carolinas. From these high slopes it meanders widely through Tennessee, Alabama, and Kentucky, where it joins the Ohio. Parts of Mississippi and Georgia contribute their waters to the wide arc of this river. There was a time, less than twenty short years ago, when the river ran wild in flood and destruction during the heavy rains of the winter. When the rains stopped falling, the river ebbed to a lazy, powerless stream. Today the Tennessee River neither destroys nor sinks into idleness. A system of man-made dams, built of concrete and steel, pierced by locks for navigation and penstocks and turbines to transform the energy of falling water into controlled and mobile electricity, has put this river to work for man.

Back on the land that forms the great valley of the Tennessee the heaviest average rainfall in the country, except for the Northwest, is being trained to run down to the river a little more slowly. After years of hard work and the practical application of the science of soil fertility by tens of thousands of farmers, grass and pastures and a revived forest cover are beginning to show green the year round. Precious topsoil, once bare and unstable under the terrific pounding of tons of raindrops, now stays in place under its green protection. Less and less does the land slip and roll into the streams and into the sea. With each year of work the people on the land are a little less at odds with the working cycles of nature, a little more sure of the future of their families.

The restoration of grass and pastures is the result in part of renewed soil fertility. New chemical processes centered about the development of electric furnaces apply the controlled energy of the river to the phosphate rock ores deposited in another geologic era. These chemical processes transform the ores into soil mineral fertilizers upon which the fertility of phosphate-deficient soils depends. Without phosphate, grass and clovers will not grow and livestock cannot be supported.

What is going on in the Tennessee Valley is in essence an adventure in faith—faith in man's ability voluntarily to achieve harmony between human pursuits in making a living and nature's fruitful habits of growth and production. Whatever success the men and women who have worked at this task can claim for their efforts, a major share of the credit must go to the day-by-day practice of a faith in the fundamental virtue of men. But, six months after my departure from the

Valley, I am more than ever concerned about the effects of fear and the lack of faith—not within the TVA but in centers of political and financial power far from the Valley. The words of my letter to the people of TVA—"Don't let little minds or the greedy intimidate or enchant you or divert you from your service to the public interest"— seem a more appropriate text for reflective comment on the continuing controversy which swirls about the Tennessee Valley Authority.

During and since the 1952 election, a new attack has been opened on the TVA under the guise of a defense of "private enterprise" against "creeping socialism." This is old stuff to that part of the American public which knows the history of the long battles about conservation and development of our great natural resources, our rivers and forests. But among the uninitiated anything called "socialism" is by that token assumed to be inimical to private enterprise. The neatness of an easy choice between black or white alternatives of doctrine frequently appeals to the uninformed; it avoids the distracting obligation to reflect about facts and the subtleties inherent in most public issues. Thus the game of pinning the "socialism" label on this great river-valley development is taken by some unsuspecting people as a call to duty. And those who have their own private reasons for discrediting TVA and all it stands for are not finicky about the means used to reach their objective.

I was made aware of this argument as a youngster in my home state of Wisconsin when the elder Bob La Follette waged his tireless campaigns—educational and political—to inform and arouse citizens about the unwise exploitation of forests and streams by the "private interest barons" of that day. And later I followed with interest the Muscle Shoals debate, which was in the 1920's—as the Dixon-Yates debate is at the time of writing—a symbol for all the issues in the controversy about the use of public lands, the development of rivers, the importance of public versus private power, and so on. My first trip to Washington, after graduation from Lawrence College, found me in the gallery of the United States Senate. There below, the floor was empty—except for one man, the great George Norris of Nebraska.

He was talking about Muscle Shoals—why it should not be sold to "private interests" but should be developed by the United States government. I knew the story, and now I was listening to Senator Norris; but his only audience in the Senate chamber was the presiding officer, and even he seemed to be asleep. To me it was an important speech; but even more significant to me was the absence of his colleagues.

The TVA is the product of a long, consistent line in the history of this country's internal argument about the conservation and use of our natural resources. Now, as for La Follette and Norris, one of the most difficult obstacles faced by those who believe in its guiding principles is in getting people to hear and believe the facts relevant to the issue. It is difficult to excuse men and women in responsible posts of government for their ignorance or their misconceptions of the subject. They reflect their lack of understanding in the important decisions they make about the future of this country's policy on river-valley development; on means of obtaining an abundant supply of electricity for the widest possible distribution at the lowest possible cost; on the methods by which our natural resources will yield their life-giving wealth for a strong economy or be butchered, bartered, or monopolized by a few to exact a higher tribute from the many.

These are important issues. To see their nature, look at the rape of the Bonneville Power Administration under the cover of glib references to "partnership"; the reopening of our few great undeveloped rivers to the scramble of competitive site-takings by piecemeal power developers in the name of "private enterprise"; the give-away of tidelands oil; and so on. And then there is the ill-conceived, poorly executed attempt to deceive the public about the real meaning of the Dixon-Yates formula, conceived as a land mine near the heart of the TVA. This conspiracy against the Authority is discussed in detail in a day and a half of testimony I gave (October 29 and 30, 1954) before the Subcommittee on Monopoly and Antitrust of the Committee on the Judiciary of the Senate.

In the heat of political debate, issues frequently are overstated. Perhaps some of the phrases I have used above illustrate the point. We need to get beneath the slogans and clichés with which issues are described. We need to study and think soberly about our natural resources and the various administrative means by which we can conserve and develop them for national benefit and strength. Doctrine, brittle and neat, is the tool of tender minds in pursuit of a policy that can be embraced without using one's intellect. Both sides in a contest for support too often feel compelled to resort to outdated and unrealistic stereotypes. In telling the story of the Tennessee Valley demonstration, I have tried to avoid doctrine. Whether or not I have succeeded must be judged by others.

In my twenty-one years in the Valley, I have seen the ideas for which La Follette, Norris, Lister Hill, and many others fought for so many discouraging years tried out in the crucible of rugged experience. As one who had been with TVA from its beginning, as a member of the staff for fourteen years and as chairman of the board for another seven, it seems important that I try to set forth in a semi-systematic way an exposition of its work. What were its motivations, its tests of experience, the significance of its decisions, as they seemed to those who helped to make them? Perhaps such a recital will help those who want to understand its real meaning, whether they indorse or reject it as good public policy; those who want to learn what the people in TVA thought they were doing, how they were trying to do it, why, and with what result.

TVA's great value to the world lies in the massive array of facts recorded and expressed in two decades of actual experience in the context of human associations among men and women of a great region, a great nation, and a troubled world. It is a demonstration of what can be done when people refuse to be intimidated or enchanted by the greedy or diverted from service to the public interest.

As we move into a new era of scientific discovery, the phrase "in the public interest" should challenge us to seek more than a greater knowledge. We must find new ways to foster co-operation in the programs of action about which men of different opinion on some things can nonetheless agree on others. The community of faith in men we build around us can stand and survive many divisions among the many things about which we differ *if only we can unite in the few things we can do together*.

The far-flung, diverse, co-operative effort the people of the Valley have built around the Tennessee Valley Authority in their own—*the public*—interest is a luminous example of success in this most difficult field of human endeavor.

G. R. C.

New York, New York
December 1954

Table of Contents

I. The TVA: An Approach to the Development of a Region

Introduction

To begin with, I shall present a somewhat general picture of the work, the purposes, and the results of the Tennessee Valley Authority, now in its twenty-first year. It is only fair to state at the outset that what I say will reflect a firm "belief in the wisdom and feasibility" of the TVA Act—a phrase contained in the oath of office of the Authority's directors.

The phrase "wisdom and feasibility," required by law as one of the tests of fitness for members of the board of directors, at once suggests that TVA is a special kind of agency with an assignment in fields where controversy is not unknown. It was a controversial subject before it was established. Controversy has beaten upon it throughout its history. And in some quarters TVA is a controversial subject today, perhaps more so than when it began. Some who opposed it did not believe it could succeed. They were against it in theory. "But why worry," they said, "it won't last long; it can't work." Some of today's opposition can be traced to a belated recognition that here was a feasible idea, indeed. So now we hear a revival of the view that it should not have been started in the first place.

But I do not intend here to debate the wisdom or feasibility of TVA. It is an existing American institution. The emulation of its approach to the development of natural resources in other parts of the world, of which there are many examples, testifies to its efficacy where the reality of resource problems is more compelling than abstract doctrine. World interest is evidence of its high export value. Some of the country's leaders who promote it as a source of exemplary suggestion for "other people" also use it as an example of questionable unorthodoxy in our domestic scene. A Valley Authority on the sacred Jordan River as a useful device for international co-operation is espoused by the same government officials who refer to its prototype at home as "creeping socialism"; an asp in the bosom at home, a dove of peace abroad.

Many of the ten thousand visitors from all over the world who have come to study the TVA development go home with a stimulating idea for which the United States gets widespread thanks. But our visitors are usually puzzled when they find it singularly alone in a country with so many great river valleys in need of attention. And once, when I attempted to explain why, our visitor smiled and told me how an Arabian monarch, intent on installing a telephone system in his desert palace against the opposition of the custodians of ancient tradition, invoked an ingenious ruse. The first trial of the Western innovation successfully relayed the message, "Allah be praised." No invention of the devil could possibly have subscribed to those words. The sacred doctrine was preserved and pragmatic values incorporated therein.

While the Tennessee Valley Authority has not been emulated in *form* within this country, the domestic value of its substance has been widely recognized. Careful students of river-valley development and of federal-state relations see abundant evidence of the steady borrowing from its lessons within this country. The comment of our Arabian friend provides a ready explanation as to why the water carried from the well of the TVA experience to nourish other river valleys is put in new bottles bearing different labels to avoid identification of the source. Perhaps there is a place in our culture for what one might call a process of "semantic immunization" to make it easier for tender and brittle minds to assimilate and use knowledge distilled from real experience.

Perhaps the subtlety of a sometimes baffling and contradictory argument which greets TVA on all sides helps to explain why its very vigorous existence seems to engender controversy. One of its unprofound friends once remarked, "I wish something could be done so that the Valley program wouldn't stir up a row every time it is on the agenda in Congress." There is a way to do this.

The formula can be very simply stated: TVA will cease to become controversial when it fails to pursue vigorously the purposes for which it was established; when it ceases to be deeply devoted to the public interest; when it gives up its persistent effort to excel in its performance of the tasks assigned to it. Should these changes occur, and the pressures and actions to bring these changes have been un-remitting since it was created, its essence as an idea and as a use-ful instrument of public service will have disappeared. TVA is con-troversial because it is consequential; let it become insignificant to the public interest, an agency of no particular account, and people will stop arguing about it.

Some of the controversy springs from deep-seated, genuine con-victions about desirable and necessary limitations upon the tendency for governmental functions to push further and further into the area of decision more properly reserved to individual citizens, to communities, and to the states. That I respect and share this concern may be evident before the end of this book.

Much of the controversy, however, is fed by resort to myth, to noisy repetition of doctrine alleged to describe the American eco-nomic system against which the TVA idea is superficially assessed. With credit to its anonymous source this couplet serves me well:

> T'aint ignorance that does the damage;
> It's knowing so much that isn't so.

For example, TVA is viewed by some as an opponent of private enter-prise. Yet in the last twenty years few regions of the country have witnessed a more rapid increase in the growth and expansion of private business than has taken place in the Tennessee Valley.

Others describe the Valley Authority as a heavy-handed extension of the powers of the federal government into the affairs of the states. The governors and agencies of the seven Valley states testify to the contrary. One frequently hears that federal funds, through this regional agency, have discouraged the development of state programs in agriculture, forestry, and water control. But, in truth, there has been a greater rate of increase in state funds applied to resource development programs in the Tennessee Valley than in the remainder of the country.

The Tennessee Valley, some allege, is a favored area, receiving larger federal aid than other regions. This is not true. A large proportion of the money provided for TVA has, in fact, gone to other parts of the country. Of the $1.4 billion it has used to buy equipment and materials, more than half, $866 million, was spent outside the Tennessee Valley states.

Figures on federal employment of civilians, grants-in-aid, military contracts, and personal income from *all* federal sources show that the Tennessee Valley is not a favored region.[1] For example, federal civilian employment in the Tennessee Valley in proportion to population is lower than in the Missouri Valley states, about equal to that in New England, and lower than in California, New York, and Illinois.

Why, then, should these myths about TVA persist?

There are undoubtedly many explanations, but I believe one of the major reasons springs from its very nature. It is a new approach to the conservation and development of the natural resources of a region by a federal agency for regional development, located in the area of its assignment. It is a government corporation, commissioned to seek a blend of federal, state, and local concerns, with re-

1. Based on a comparative analysis of the Additional Reports of the Joint Committee on Reduction of Nonessential Federal Expenditures, *Federal Grants-in-Aid to States* (Senate Doc. 101 [82d Cong., 2d sess. (Washington, D.C., 1952)]), Table 4; *Federal Civilian Employment, 1950* (Committee Print [82d Cong., 1st sess. (Washington, D.C., 1950)]); and income estimates derived from United States Department of Commerce data and other sources; prime contracts as reported by the Munitions Board; and employment estimates based on reports of the Bureau of Labor Statistics and Civil Service Commission.

sponsibility defined in fairly specific terms. It is held to a strict accounting for results, yet it is without authority to prescribe and enforce a plan.

The subject matter of its work includes a good cross-section of the controversial issues inherent in the development of resources anywhere in the United States. The very nature of the problems or subjects it touches has, throughout our history, been subject to controversy—about the necessity or desirability of the objective, about the methods by which the result should be obtained, and about who should get the benefits. Who should get the benefits—there's the rub. This is true for most administrative assignments whether in the domain of private or public activity. But controversy can be especially sharp when the subject matter is land, water, forests, minerals, chemical fertilizers, and electric energy. For in these fields, as President Franklin D. Roosevelt pointed out in April, 1933, in his message to Congress requesting legislation to establish TVA, what is proposed "touches and gives life to all forms of human concerns."

As the federal Executive Branch is organized, the problems of resource development traditionally are divided among a large family of departments, bureaus, and offices. Each one has a part of the resource development assignment; each one has a special clientele whose interests are directly related to only a part of the whole. The stage is thus set for each bureau to keep peace with its own clientele. Conflicting interests, strong and real in the region where the resources exist, are not resolved locally; they come together for solution in the nation's capital, sometimes obscured or grossly distorted by lack of reliable information about the facts. One might almost say that these features of our federal organization encourage the convergence of special-interest groups on the capital and at times greatly increase the means by which they can enforce their will.

Precision of fit between problem and proposal, a difficult task at best, is made more difficult under these circumstances. The heavy mortality of factual analyses and professional judgments in the process of long-distance sifting and screening is tragic. Compromise on top of a whole series of compromises follows. The result is a policy and program frequently wide of the mark.

A regional agency has to face these conflicting interests within the region. TVA, having a wide variety of basic responsibilities relating to land, water, forests, and electric power, must do its best to resolve these conflicts within the region and present an integrated justification for its actions and suggestions—or fail.

That TVA has succeeded more than it has failed is perhaps the main reason why it continues to be controversial. Its continued existence as a regional agency, able and willing to act and to mobilize the active support and understanding of a large majority of people of the region, is a challenge to the administrative methods and the jurisdictions of established national bureaucracies.

That it continues to be controversial is testimony also to the tenacity of public interest in the problems and promise of our natural resources. In this sense TVA is a stimulant to public discussion, a laboratory for experiment, a demonstration of the hazardous but fruitful relationship between management and politics where the lines of responsibility in each field are kept discernibly clear—clear enough to permit the public to know who did what and whom to hold accountable for what happened.

Some Historical Background

The work of TVA began in 1933. In May of that year the United States Congress enacted, and President Franklin D. Roosevelt signed, the Tennessee Valley Authority Act. This act created a government corporation which, in the words of the chairman of the House committee in charge of this legislation, was "charged with the duty of constantly *studying the whole situation* presented by Tennessee River Valley, and the adjoining territory, with the view of encouraging and guiding in the orderly and *balanced development* of the diverse and rich *resources* of that section."[2]

2. *Muscle Shoals* (House Report 48 [73d Cong., 1st sess. (Washington, D.C., 1933)]), pp. 10–11. (Italics mine.)

This new approach of balanced or unified development of natural resources has a long history.[3] In the fast-moving world of today the background of events tends to become blurred in the public mind. In the twenty years in which TVA has been operating, a whole new generation has grown up; it can have no direct recollection of the fifteen-year controversy prior to 1933 over the disposition of the Muscle Shoals properties of World War I out of which came the germ of the Valley Authority idea. It is a generation unfamiliar with the then-famous offer by Henry Ford to buy the Muscle Shoals nitrate plants and lease Wilson Dam—one of the many proposals carefully analyzed in a history of the Muscle Shoals issue written by Judson King, a still valiant champion of conservation.[4] Today's generation is unfamiliar with the long debates which led Congress to choose from a welter of legislative proposals on the subject—138 in all—and, twice before 1933, to pass legislation providing for government operation of the Muscle Shoals properties and the development of the Tennessee River Basin. Both bills were vetoed. President Coolidge used the pocket veto to kill a Muscle Shoals bill passed by a Republican Congress; clearly he was against it, but for reasons unstated. President Hoover's veto message was not ambiguous.

Two generations have grown up since the turn of the century, when such conservationists as Gifford Pinchot, an American forester trained in Europe, and W J McGee, a geologist and hydrologist, joined with President Theodore Roosevelt in initiating the "Conservation Movement." They gave voice to the idea that "a river is essentially a unit from its source to the sea" and ought to be developed for "all

3. See "The Historical Roots of TVA," in *Annual Report of the Tennessee Valley Authority, 1953* (1953), pp. 51–52.

4. "From July 1921 to May 1933 there were no less than 138 bills introduced in Congress affecting the disposition of Muscle Shoals. Many of these embodied the proposals of private power or chemical companies or other industralists; the others were general leasing bills or proposals for outright public operation" (Judson King, *The Legislative History of Muscle Shoals* [Knoxville: Tennessee Valley Authority, 1936], III, 127).

of the uses of the waters and benefits to be derived from their control."[5]

Thus the concepts which found their way into the TVA Act written in 1933 had their beginnings many years before. That Franklin D. Roosevelt of New York was in the White House in 1933, George Norris of Nebraska was in the Senate, and the country was prostrate with unemployment had almost everything to do with its creation at that time. But the ideas and policies written into the Act evolved from the reflective observations, studies, and experience of the scientists and the informed concern of laymen who initiated the conservation movement.

In historical perspective it is clear that none of the responsibilities assigned to the Valley Authority was new to the federal government. For decades the federal government had been carrying on projects for the development and use of water power, for navigation, and for control of floods; it had established laboratories for the improvement of minerals processing, for use of forest resources, and for the improvement and testing of fertilizers. Nor was TVA endowed with any new governmental powers.

The TVA Act and Its Purposes

What was new was the administrative device. The Act created, according to President Roosevelt, "a corporation clothed with the power of government but possessed of the flexibility and initiative of a private enterprise."[6]

A summary of its far-reaching purposes is found in Section 23 of the Act:

for the especial purpose of bringing about in said Tennessee drainage basin and adjoining territory . . . (1) the maximum amount of flood control; (2) the maximum development . . . for navigation purposes; (3) the maximum

5. *Report of the National Conservation Commission* . . . (Senate Doc. 676 [60th Cong., 2d sess. (Washington, D.C., 1909)]), I, 45, 47.

6. *Muscle Shoals Development* (House Doc. 15 [73d Cong., 1st sess. (Washington, D.C., 1933)]), p. 1.

generation of electric power consistent with flood control and navigation; (4) the proper use of marginal lands; (5) the proper method of reforestation . . . and (6) the economic and social well-being of the people living in said river basin.[7]

To this list should be added the extremely important responsibility: "to provide for the national defense."

The assignment was a big one, with great and complex responsibilities—quite enough for any one organization. But one should not regard the assignment as larger or more inclusive than it actually is. There are some, of course, who attempt to do so; thence comes the attempt to stigmatize the Authority as a "superstate" or to invest it with imaginary powers as an economic dictator for an entire region.

TVA's responsibility in the Valley region—an area about one and a half times the size of New England—is confined largely to the development of resources and their use. And development of resources is but one part—a fundamental part, to be sure—of comprehensive development. By contrast, a program for economic development might include many activities which are outside the scope of its task and responsibilities; for example, responsibility for money and banking policies, tax and fiscal matters, tariffs, social welfare programs, public investments in roads, schools, and hospitals, transportation rates and policies, agricultural affairs, immigration and emigration, and many other governmental activities which will vary with the contingencies of particular times and places.

TVA does not even have exclusive responsibility within the Valley region in the field of resource development. It has not supplanted, but rather has supplemented, the activities of other federal, state, and local agencies, which continue to exercise virtually all their traditional responsibilities. Its special function is to see the resource base in its entirety, to view the interrelationship among the various resources, and to guide and encourage development in the light of that insight.

Later, in chapter iv, "TVA and the States," I shall describe the methods it uses in co-operating with agencies of the states and the

7. Act of May 18, 1933, Sec. 23 (48 Stat. 69).

federal government. This will make it clear that it invites use of their specialized skills, facilities, and organization. In agriculture, for example, its expenditures since 1933 have totaled perhaps one-tenth of all federal funds used in the Valley by all agencies for agricultural development activities of one kind or another. Many more illustrations could be cited. For one other example, its dams have provided opportunities for the United States Fish and Wildlife Service and state conservation agencies to establish bird and game refuges along the shore lines of the new lakes.

There is another myth about TVA which is very easy for well-informed people to believe. That is the notion that it was set up as a special concession to a single, small region and that this region has reaped the benefits while the taxpayers of the rest of the nation bear the expense. This view asserts that the Valley Authority was set up in the Tennessee Valley region because it was a depressed area, needing special aid on the part of the federal government.

True, the area was in bad straits—and so was the rest of the country. But TVA was established for more than regional or local benefit. Federal funds were invested in this area, just as other activities of the federal government are carried on in other limited regions, for the national benefit. Although it operates largely in a specific region, it is, in fact, a national enterprise "for the general social and economic welfare of the Nation," as President Roosevelt stated in his message to Congress.[8] Moreover, some of its responsibilities extend outside the region. It helps to control floods on the lower Ohio and Mississippi. Its program of fertilizer research, experimental production, and demonstration, while small in amount of expenditure, is national in scope. It contributes to the national defense through munitions research and production and the generation of great quantities of power for the production of chemicals, aluminum, and titanium and for the atomic-energy program. Atomic-energy plants are its largest customers. By 1955 at least one-half of TVA's power production—the largest power system in the world—will go to the atomic-energy facilities of the United States government.

8. *Muscle Shoals Development*, p. 1.

In 1933 the entire country was in the throes of a depression. This may have struck with greater force in the Tennessee Valley and the Southeast generally because of the return of many of its people from northern industrial centers where their jobs had disappeared. But this was not the main reason for choosing the Tennessee Valley for the experiment in a new approach to resource development.

With a growing national interest in conservation measures, and with idle World War I facilities at Muscle Shoals as a starting point, the Tennessee River Basin presented an unusual opportunity to rebuild a whole river and its watershed. The notion that this region was especially favored by the federal government is nourished most by those who would persuade other regions to adopt "anything but a TVA" on the hypothetical ground that only poor regions need so drastic a remedy. And few self-respecting regions will admit to that description!

The development of other streams and other regions has gone forward, not in response to pleas of help from destitute people. Federal dams have been built on the Columbia River in the Pacific Northwest, giant dams and reservoirs dot the vast Missouri Valley, and more are being built. In the Ohio Valley multipurpose works for flood control and other purposes continue to be added. The Colorado is in part harnessed by the great Hoover Dam, the tallest in the world.

In all these regions, as in the Tennessee Valley, huge federal expenditures are being made. If that is favoritism, let us recognize it as favoritism for the strength and welfare of the American people.

TVA as a Method of Integration and Decentralization

The role of TVA in the Tennessee Valley is twofold. It has undertaken and carried out the program of physical construction and operation to put the river to work—a task of the federal government too great and too broad in scope to be accomplished by private organizations or by state or local agencies of government. In addition, it has provided the unifying influence, the sense of cohesion and direction, essential to a comprehensive program for conservation and development. By stimulating the interest of state and local agencies close to the people, it has opened new avenues for joint action, strengthening rather than weakening state and local initiative. A brief description of TVA as an organization and its methods of work will make this clear.

In form it is a government corporation endowed with some of the flexibility of a private corporation. It is headed by a board of three directors appointed by the President and confirmed by the United States Senate. The President designates one of the three directors as chairman of the board. A general manager, appointed by the board, heads the staff, comprising civil, electrical, and chemical engineers; biologists; experts in public health, forestry, agriculture, political science, and economics; managers; and so on. At the peak of World War II, when TVA was building twelve dams at once to expand power supply for aluminum and atomic energy, its forces grew to more than forty thousand men and women. Today, in 1954, it employs about twenty-two thousand people, about half of them in construction—for we still build to keep power supply in pace with the growth of the region and the requirements of national defense.

TVA is dependent upon Congress for annual appropriations required to finance activities of public benefit; these are traditional functions of the federal government, but they do not produce revenues for the Authority. Among these nonrevenue-producing activities, most of them carried on in co-operation with more than a hundred state and local agencies, are flood control, navigation and research, experiments and demonstrations helpful to soil-fertility conservation, agricultural and industrial development, and the fuller use of all the resources of the Valley.

As the sole source of elecricity for an entire region, and to assure the taxpayers a fair return on their investment, TVA is authorized by law to use its receipts from the sale of power in the conduct of its power business. This wise provision, customary in business and corporate practice, helps to make it possible to satisfy the expanding energy requirements of the area and to serve new needs and new customers promptly. But, like all other utilities, net earnings alone, particularly in a period of rapid expansion, do not provide enough capital to build new power plants. As a utility obtains capital by selling stock and borrowing money, so TVA goes to Congress to seek more capital for power expansion. All the money appropriated to it for power facilities is repayable to the government; the Authority is already paying back this money well ahead of schedule.

TVA is fully accountable to the President and to Congress for what it does and the way it performs its work. This accountability is achieved by full and complete audits of its financial records; by hearings each year before the Bureau of the Budget, acting for the President, and by hearings before the appropriations committees of Congress; by review and examination of all its activities before congressional committees; and by periodic reports to Congress, the President, and the public. TVA is subject to an even more penetrating scrutiny and accountability through its day-by-day work with the people and the agencies of the state and local governments in the Valley. In the next chapter I shall discuss the meaning of this word "accountability" in the story of how men and management rebuilt a river—twenty dams in twenty years.

Natural resources do not conform to man-made boundaries. The watershed of the Tennessee River includes parts of seven states. The fact that much of the developmental action must come from the separate state governments or institutions in several states has not proved an insurmountable obstacle; on the contrary, this circumstance is a fortunate invitation to joint planning and consultation.

The full development of a region for the benefit of human living depends as much upon the administrative or managerial resources of the region as it does upon the human and physical resources. The creation of the Authority established a new administrative resource in the Tennessee Valley to help the states to work together. The job in this respect is to see to it that the facts about the wise use of our resources of water, soils, minerals, and factors of climate are discovered and made available to become a part of the everyday voluntary decisions of people. This will be discussed further in chapter iv, "TVA and the States."

Two Major Resource Problems of the Tennessee Valley

There was need for much joint counsel and planning with the people of the Valley when the Authority began its work. The full development of the natural resources of the region in the national interest faced two fundamental handicaps which pervaded the physical setting, depressed the economy, and restricted the freedom of the people.

For more than a century the Tennessee River had been identified as a stream of great undeveloped and wasted power, a potential inland waterway, but a destroyer of life and property as it ran in flood year after year. American capital, private and public, passed it by and chose instead to invest in other regions. Those who urged the enactment of the TVA Act apparently believed that, if the Tennessee River were conquered and its water power harnessed, the river would help transform the economic life of the region and increase the productive capacity of the nation. Nothing less than the resources of the United States government could cope with this task.

The second handicap which plagued the region was closely related to, if not part and parcel of, the wasted river. The Tennessee Valley has more rainfall than any other region in the country except the Pacific Northwest. Because of its temperate climate, it has a longer growing season than most other large areas of the country. It has abundant rainfall and a growing season in more effective combination than any other region of comparable size in the country, without exception. But these priceless natural assets of moderate sunshine and abundant rain had been used too little. Sunshine, soil, water, and human beings were not working together.

The agriculture of the region emphasized cultivation of row crops, principally corn and cotton. There are many reasons why this was done; one was the lack of soil minerals, especially phosphate, required to nourish a grass and animal agriculture. Reliance upon corn and cotton left the land idle and uncovered during what could have been a winter growing season, the period of the heavy rains. Wasted rain and wasted sunshine were serious losses in themselves. In addition, year by year, the fertility of the soil and the soil itself washed away.

And the wealth of the soil captured in cotton seed, for example, was largely exported from the region never to return to the lands of the Valley.

Under these conditions a low level of productivity prevailed throughout the region. Few raw materials were produced for industry's use, and most of these were carried through only the simpler types of processing. This arrangement brought small return to the people of the Valley. In 1929, before the depression, the per capita income of the Tennessee Valley was only 44 per cent of the national average. Wasted water, wasted soil, and wasted sunshine depressed economic opportunity at home, and men and women were forced to migrate from the Tennessee Valley to work in the factories of other regions.

These, in brief, are some of the problems which helped to define TVA's assignment. The problems of the Tennessee Valley marked this region as a good place to apply modern engineering theories to a whole river and combine that development with the inseparable problem of conservation on the land.[9]

TVA and the River

The Tennessee River (see Fig. 1) has its principal headwaters in the Appalachian Mountains of Virginia and North Carolina. Ranked by volume of stream flow, it is the fifth largest river system in the United States. The Mississippi, Columbia, and Ohio outrank It; the muddy flow of the Missouri barely exceeds the Tennessee. The main stem of the river forms at Knoxville, Tennessee, where two of its major tributaries join—the Holston River from southwestern Virginia and the French Broad from western North Carolina. Its course goes southwest through eastern Tennessee, gathering the flow of important tributaries: the Clinch carrying water from southwestern Virginia,

9. For a brief but authoritative analysis of the evolution of law, engineering, and national policy in conservation of water resources see J. L. Fly, "The Role of the Federal Government in the Conservation and Utilization of Water Resources," *University of Pennsylvania Law Review*, LXXXVI (January, 1938), 274–94.

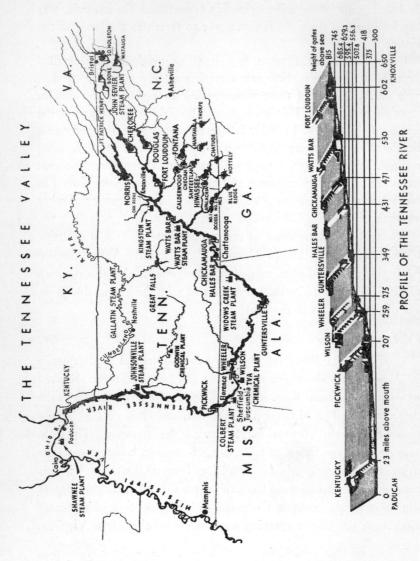

PROFILE OF THE TENNESSEE RIVER

Fig. 1

the Little Tennessee from North Carolina, and the Hiwassee and Ocoee rivers, whose headwaters are in North Carolina and Georgia.

Thus grown, the Tennessee flows into the northern part of Alabama. Here it turns north and west, crosses that state, and swings north through western Tennessee and Kentucky. Some 630 miles from Knoxville it joins the Ohio River to flow on into the Mississippi River at Cairo, Illinois. The stream flow of the Tennessee accounts for some 25 per cent of the Ohio's discharge into the Mississippi. The watershed of the Tennessee River is about 40,000 square miles.

This is the river than once wasted its great power in destruction of land, property, and human life. Today, the Tennessee River is the most completely controlled major river system in the United States. The integrated development of the Tennessee River and its tributaries has provided flood control, navigation facilities, and power at less cost than could have been achieved by single-purpose developments.

The present TVA system of dams and reservoirs provides nearly 12,000,000 acre-feet of storage for flood control at the beginning of the flood season each year. In the seventeen years since Norris Dam was placed in operation, the reservoir system has prevented approximately $45 million of flood damage at one city alone, Chattanooga, Tennessee. On the lower Ohio and Mississippi rivers, this system can reduce flood crests by $2\frac{1}{2}$–3 feet, depending on the origin of the flood. This provides protection to 6,000,000 acres of rich bottom land outside the Tennessee Valley and will lessen the frequency of flooding on another 4,000,000 acres. When you hear about the several hundred thousands of acres TVA has permanently flooded in the Tennessee Valley to provide the reservoirs behind its dams, think of these millions of acres protected outside the region.

A 630-mile navigation channel has been created on which new traffic records are being set regularly. In the past year the new channel carried more than a billion ton-miles of freight. This was an increase of more than thirty fold compared with river traffic before TVA began to improve the river. Formerly, the major traffic consisted of sand and gravel dredged from the river bed and hauled short

distances and of forest products moved by barge. Now the modernized river—a chain of lakes joined together by single-lift locks—
carries products of higher value, such as coal, oil, grain, and steel, and
for longer distances, frequently between the Valley and the Middle
West. In addition to the substantial annual savings in transportation
costs afforded by the new waterway, now amounting to some $10
million a year, it proved itself to be a valuable asset in supplementing
railroad facilities during the last war.

The same dams which control flood waters and provide a channel
for navigation also produce hydroelectricity. TVA's electric-power
system now generates twenty-three times as much electricity as the
area produced in 1933—over 35,000,000,000 kilowatt-hours of energy
annually for one and one-third million consumers over a territory of
80,000 square miles. The electricity sold from the same system of
dams brings the government a return which has averaged more than
4 per cent annually on the investment in power facilities. The return on the investment, after depreciation and payments in lieu of
taxes to states and counties, certifies a financial performance well
beyond the original objective of a self-liquidating power system prescribed in the basic Act.

There is much more to the story than the earning record of TVA's
power system. The power operations of TVA and the one hundred
and fifty municipal and rural electric co-operative partners that distribute its electricity have stimulated neighboring private utilities
in many ways. In the two concluding chapters, devoted to the important subject of adequate power supply for the nation's needs—
about which the private utilities and the government are still doing too
little—we shall go into this matter in some detail.

Electricity in greater abundance on the farms and in the homes and
factories of the Tennessee Valley has helped to spark a great economic
change. Per capita income, as one index of that change, is now 61 per
cent of the national average, compared with 44 per cent in the boom
year of 1929. Higher incomes in the Tennessee Valley have contributed to the economic life of the nation. For example, that part of

the nation's total of individual federal income taxes which comes from the seven Valley states has steadily increased. In 1933 individual federal income taxes from the seven states were 3.4 per cent of the total of such taxes in the nation. In 1952 they were 6.2 per cent of the national total. Thus the states of which the Tennessee Valley region is a part are sharing more of the common burden of the costs of government.

TVA and the People on the Land

The fundamental handicap in the use of the region's soils, its abundant rainfall, and its life-giving sunshine is also slowly being corrected in a far-reaching program of education and experiment. TVA's chemical plants at Muscle Shoals, built during the first World War, have been modernized. They contributed heavily to the requirements of the United States and its allies for munitions and other war needs during World War II. These plants are now used, as they were before the war, to develop and produce new and improved fertilizers, mainly high-analysis phosphates and nitrates. The fertilizer materials produced are significant, not for the volume produced, but for the way they are used. Appendix A, "Farms, Fertilizers, and Munitions," will describe the regional and national contribution made by this World War I inheritance.

It may be enough now to point out that, as electricity and machines have moved into the rural areas and as grass, pastures, and livestock have substituted more of the sun's energies for human backbreaking toil, the land has released a new surplus of human energy. Hundreds of thousands of people within the Valley have found new employment opportunities in the towns and cities. The number of people employed in nonfarm activities has almost doubled in the Tennessee Valley and in TVA's power service area since the prosperity year of 1929. From 1929 to 1954 the net gain in manufacturing plants has numbered more than two thousand, representing a rate of increase considerably greater than the rate of increase for the nation as a whole during the same period. These new enterprises are additions to the productive resources of the region and the nation. Less than a dozen, and all of these small, have moved from other areas of the country to the Tennessee Valley; the remainder are newly created additions to the nation's productive capacity.

This, in brief, is the summary of physical and economic change in the Tennessee Valley since TVA began its work. The task of full development of the region is not finished; it is only well begun.

We view the full development of the Tennessee Valley as something more than mobilization of economic assets for the achievement of greater material rewards. The Tennessee Valley's greatest asset is its people—people who generally prefer to live there because they like its hills and valleys, its mountains and forests, its prevailing sense of community, and the depth of the region's cultural roots and traditions. Characterize this as sentiment, and you miss the point. Because, when men and women find productive and satisfying work and exercise their initiative freely where they *prefer* to live, the results reach far beyond the dollar value of their labor. Under these circumstances people gain a new birth of freedom, and the world gains new wealth in goods, ideas, and human self-respect.

II. Men and Management Rebuild a River

Introduction

Money, materials, machines, and men are the basic ingredients in building a dam. And the greatest of these is men.

The Tennessee Valley Authority has built twenty dams in twenty years. These dams represent more than one-half billion dollars. One hundred and thirteen million cubic yards of concrete, rock, and earth fill, twelve times the bulk of the seven great pyramids of Egypt, have been used to build these structures into the river bed of the Tennessee and its tributaries. Almost two hundred thousand different men and women at one time or another have been employed by TVA for a direct part in this colossal job.

Construction work in any season in any climate cannot put comfort above achievement. But, if the planners, builders, and managers know and have faith in men, they will contrive to make the process of construction satisfying to those who do the work—a theater for the kind of creative experience in which men build themselves as they build a dam.

TVA has built these twenty dams in twenty years with its own employees. Each structure was placed, designed, and built to serve a purpose peculiar to itself. Taken together, they form a unit for the control and productivity of a great river system. There is Fontana Dam—fourth largest and fourth highest in the world—rising 480 feet above bedrock in a canyon of the North Carolina mountains. There is Kentucky Dam, near the mouth of the Tennessee River as it flows into the Ohio near Paducah, more than a mile and a half long, with two-thirds of its concrete bulk invisible, reaching down 100 feet through soft overburden to the solid limestone rock. Kentucky Dam's foundations are especially designed to withstand earthquakes such as the one which occurred near by and changed the course of the Mississippi more than a hundred years ago. The shore line of the 184-mile-long lake behind Kentucky Dam, if straightened out, would reach from Chicago to Los Angeles. This great reservoir can regulate the full flow of a flooded Tennessee River to reduce flood crests on the lower Ohio and Mississippi.

More figures could be given—I could illustrate the size of these operations by pointing out that the 22,000,000 acre-feet of water which can be stored behind TVA's dams could cover the entire state of Illinois to a depth of 8 inches. But these dams were not built to create impressive statistics. They were built to carry out the purposes specified by the United States Congress in the Tennessee Valley Authority Act of 1933. They were built to control the devastating floods of a river whose annual discharge nearly equals that of the Missouri, to provide a new inland waterway for the benefit of our national commerce. These dams were built to turn the potential electrical energy of the untamed river into the push buttons and motors of more than a million-and-a-quarter homes and industries.

While TVA placed concrete and erected steel, it also built a greater asset—an organization of men and women—a demonstration of achievement within the public service which people from all over the world have come to see. Tens of thousands of men and women have acquired new skills, a new understanding of the utility of the resources of their Valley, a new faith in the strength of co-operation to achieve collectively what no one of them could accomplish alone.

How this kind of organization came into being, how it was built to promote among employees a sense of individual responsibility and to elicit good performance beyond the minimum requirements of the wage contract, will become clear as the record is recited.

Dams, Deadlines, and People

The construction of a dam involves a careful fit of a whole new landscape into the economy and ways of life of the surrounding area. In the process of building these dams and planting in the powerhouses the quiet hum of electric energy, 15,000 families were obliged to move from the backwater areas which had to be flooded. Flowage rights or full ownership had to be purchased covering 35,000 tracts of land comprising about a million acres. More than 19,000 graves were moved to new places of rest; 170 schoolhouses, 180 churches, and, in some instances, whole towns and villages were relocated or physically reorganized to make way for the lakes behind the dams.

Roads, railroads, and bridges were the subject of negotiation, agreements, equitable transactions, involving private corporations, county courts, and state and federal agencies. Owners, congregations, nearest of kin, village councils, whoever and whatever had a right or a reason to be consulted or considered in making the new shore line an accepted and acceptable part of the landscape, were involved in the result. For every cubic yard of concrete and every ton of steel now solidly fused into TVA's dams there were dozens of transactions among people, involving family history, the future of communities, the plans of the local and state agencies, the use of the new lakes, and the power to be extracted from these new waters by the magic of the dynamo.

Every one of these tens of thousands of transactions and agreements had to proceed under a schedule that was determined by the date the reservoir was scheduled to begin filling. While concrete was being placed at the dam site, land-buyers, family-relocation specialists, reservoir timber-clearance crews, surveyors relocating railroad and highway lines, even technicians from the universities excavating the artifacts from ancient Indian mounds—all who had part in this complex task—were working under deadlines. They were deadlines dictated by water and weather but determined by TVA's engineers to make efficient use of the taxpayers' dollars.

Experienced engineers must schedule the tempo of a dam's construction to bring each major stage of the structure to the point where floods or winter rains cannot hinder the work or undo what has been done. It takes cost-conscious engineering to fit the separate construction operations together so that the new dam will be ready to hold back the seasonal floods and convert their force into use and revenue.

If a dam is ready before the seasonal stream flow comes to fill the reservoir, months of idle investment add to the cost of the dam. If the gates of the dam are not ready to be closed when the heavy flows come, flood control is delayed and power revenues are lost. Weeks and days, according to seasons, count heavily in the economy of re-building a river.

And it takes a kind of skill in human persuasion, too. A family living in a mountain cove miles away from the river might not believe that their home would be submerged by a definite date just because their property lay below the white-staked contour line set by a TVA sur-vey party. More than once it was necessary to persuade such families to visit a dam already built, to show them the lake, and by map to ex-plain the inevitable course of water along a contour, fixed by the height of a dam many miles and ridges away. If a single family remained below the contour lines the water would reach by a certain date, the time gained and the money saved by managerial and engineering skill at the site of the dam would be lost. A new, unfilled reservoir had to be-come a deserted land, a cleared land with buildings and debris removed or wired to the ground or burned, with new roads and bridges built above the future shore line.

In one instance during the war the gates on a new dam were ready to be closed when the last remaining family, ready to move to a new farm location, was delayed. An aged grandfather was suddenly stricken with pneumonia. To move him invited grave risk. Special medical aid availed nothing. But, while there was life, the closure of the dam was postponed. Building dams is more than putting together rock and earth, concrete and steel.

These may seem to be small details, but I mention them for a special reason. They are, perhaps, illustrations of a special kind of accounta-bility for a human result, going far beyond engineering precision, that recurs again and again in any fair recital of TVA's work. No greater testimony can be found to demonstrate the rejection of autocratic methods, the high skill of the organization as a builder, and the concern for human rights and dignity of this government agency than the fact that the people of the Tennessee Valley have come to cherish TVA as an institution among them. Indeed, they have risen up on many occasions to protect it from the not infrequent attempts to dilute or destroy its competence, its integrity, and its scope of service.

Strict Accountability for Results

Those who would find a simple answer to the record of achievement of TVA in these last twenty years, would not be far wrong if they went back to 1908, when President Theodore Roosevelt transmitted to Congress the report of the historic Inland Waterways Commission. In that message President Roosevelt criticized the "piecemeal execution of projects" which characterized the country's approach to the development of our rivers, the rehabilitation and conservation of our soils and forests, and urged that a new method be considered. He said, "We shall not succeed [in making] the best use of our rivers or for exercising foresight in their development . . . until the responsibility for administering the policy and executing and extending the plan is definitely laid on one man or group of men who can be held accountable."[1]

President Franklin D. Roosevelt, in his message to Congress in April, 1933, requesting legislation to create a Tennessee Valley Authority, called for "a corporation clothed with the power of government but possessed of the flexibility and initiative of a private enterprise," a development that "touches and gives life to all forms of human concerns."[2] Here, indeed, was a special kind of accountability for a special kind of result.

The managers of the House of Representatives who sat with Senate conferees said this in their conference report on the TVA Bill as it went to the floor for debate and later adoption:

We are fully persuaded that the full success of the Tennessee Valley development project will depend more upon the ability, vision, and executive

1. *Preliminary Report of the Inland Waterways Commission* (Senate Doc. 325 [60th Cong., 1st sess. (Washington, D.C., 1908)]), p. 5.

2. *Muscle Shoals Development* (House Doc. 15 [73d Cong., 1st sess. (Washington, D.C., 1933)]), p. 1.

capacity of the members of the board than upon legislative provisions. We have sought to set up a legislative framework, but not to encase it in a legislative strait jacket. We intend that the corporation shall have much of the essential freedom and elasticity of a private business corporation. We have indicated the course it shall take, but have not directed the particular steps it shall make.[3]

The "flexibility and initiative" and "freedom and elasticity" of a private business enterprise are capable of as many interpretations as there are kinds of private enterprises. Certainly the phrases suggest an expected efficiency, economy, and dependable performance and discretion in choice of methods.

Those who would understand TVA and attempt to appraise its record of service would be well advised to read and study the Act from beginning to end in the light of the above quotations.[4] It is a significant document. It sets forth the assignments intrusted to this new kind of agency located in the region of its work and specifies its purposes and the expectations for great development the framers of the Act envisioned when they wrote it and pressed for its enactment.

Many specific policies were settled and decided by the law. It was TVA's task to make these policies come to life in the hands of a responsible organization of men and women. The administrative provisions of the Act are, in my judgment, most important. Section 3 authorizes the board of three directors, appointed by the President and confirmed by the Senate, to build its organization outside the civil service laws, rules, and regulations and to create "an organization to fix responsibility and promote efficiency." Then, unlike most congressional enactments placing agencies outside the civil service, the Act contains Section 6, which I quote in full, for it has been the solid rock upon which there has been built a responsible organization accountable to the public for the results of its performance and not for the way its employees vote:

3. *Operation of Muscle Shoals Properties, Etc.* (House Report 130 [73d Cong., 1st sess. (Washington, D.C., 1933)]), p. 19.

4. See Appendix B for the full text of the TVA Act.

In the appointment of officials and the selection of employees for said Corporation, and in the promotion of any such employees or officials, no political test or qualification shall be permitted or given consideration, but all such appointments and promotions shall be given and made on the basis of merit and efficiency. Any member of said board who is found by the President of the United States to be guilty of a violation of this section shall be removed from office by the President of the United States, and any appointee of said board who is found by the board to be guilty of a violation of this section shall be removed from office by said board.[5]

Other provisions of the Act make TVA responsible for the purchase and sale of land as required in carrying out the purposes of the Act, give it power to sue and to be sued in courts of the land, authorize the board to use surplus revenues in the conduct of its business, and provide for annual reports to the President and to the Congress, including detailed financial statements set forth and audited in the manner common among businessmen.

These and other detailed provisions fix responsibility and allow a high degree of freedom from remote controls and hidden veto powers which might be exercised by other agencies. The Act couples these delegations with a measure of strict accountability for the results expected to flow from the enactment of the law.

In a recent statement Senator Hill of Alabama recalled the intent of those members of the House and Senate legislative committees as they met in conference as managers for their respective houses to resolve the differences between the two bodies and produce the TVA Act as signed by the President. That group included Senator George Norris of Nebraska, whose persistent efforts in the 1920's led the way to this occasion. Senator Hill, then a member of the House, is the only member of the Congress today who can report that historic moment in the process of the bill's enactment. He said:

We sought, in the original act, to give one agency responsibility for Federal leadership in the development of all the resources of one river valley, to locate its management in the region, close to the problem and out of Washington, to make it responsible directly to the President and to the Congress. Those were

5. Act of May 18, 1933, Sec. 6 (48 Stat. 63).

new ways to approach the age-old task of trying to develop wisely and fully the resources of nature for the well-being of man.

We tried, in creating a Government corporation, to free TVA, insofar as a public agency can be freed, from red tape, from the ailments of bureaucracy. We tried to couple authority with responsibility so that we could hold the Board accountable for results. We tried to eliminate the chance for buck-passing, for the alibis which prevent the fixing of responsibility and frustrate accomplishment in the traditional fragmentation of Federal programs. We set out specific goals for TVA to accomplish, but we left to management determination of the way to do it.[6]

Building the TVA Organization

Many decisions full of the seeds of precedent confronted the TVA board immediately upon taking over its responsibilities. High on the list was the choice of a plan and a method for mobilizing an organization and, second, and concurrently, selection of an engineering plan for an early start on the construction of dams on the Tennessee River.

In beginning its work to rebuild the river, the Authority had wide latitude for important decisions, restricted, however, by two instructions in the law. First, that a navigable channel 9 feet in depth must be provided for the 650 miles from the mouth of the river to Knoxville, the head of navigation. Second, that all planning and operation must give priority to navigation and flood control over all other purposes, including the production of power.

In the face of this assignment, the board had to decide what engineering plan to follow. At the time the TVA Bill was being considered by the Congress in 1933, there was available an extensive report which had been complied by the Army Corps of Engineers prior to 1931. This report included a scheme of thirty-two low navigation dams and locks for the main channel of the Tennessee. These dams would provide no flood control and no power. An alternative scheme contained in the same report proposed a system of nine high dams, including the Wilson Dam and the Hales Bar Dam already built. The

6. United States Congress, Senate, *Second Independent Offices Appropriations for 1954: Hearings before Subcommittee of the Committee on Appropriations . . . on H.R. 5690* (83d Cong., 1st sess. [Washington, D.C.: Government Printing Office, 1953]), pp. 421–22.

high-dam scheme would create the 9-foot navigation channel and also provide for flood control and power. With these alternatives counterposed, with TVA still unborn, the Army Engineers had already secured initial appropriations and begun work on the lock for the first of a compromise system of about twelve intermediate-size dams, consistent with neither of the alternatives recommended in their report.

The Act, as adopted, embraced the high-dam scheme by indirection, for engineering logic inexorably asserted that the maximum amount of flood control, navigation, and power could be achieved only by the construction of high dams properly spaced along the river and its tributaries. TVA began to develop plans for a system of high, multiple-purpose dams. This choice required plans and designs that would use the same space in reservoirs for both flood control and power, a policy deprecated by many prominent engineers of that day. In recruiting engineers to give life to this idea—multiple-purpose dams—those who believed in the feasibility of this approach were sought and found.

As TVA built its organization of engineers, competent to plan, to design, and to rebuild the river, it faced another decision—one among many, to be sure, but one of great importance for the Authority as it is today: How should these great dams be built? Should they be let out to contract, as was customary, or should the board of directors organize its own forces and go to work? To employ contractors requires bids, and a sound bidding procedure requires advance preparation of basic designs and detailed specifications covering thousands of particulars. Building a dam by contract, in fact, is to build a dam at least twice, once on the drawing board before a cubic yard of dirt is moved and building it again on the site. Sometimes it is built a third time—in the courts to adjudicate responsibility for the changes made between original specifications and the structural details and contents as finally built. There are short cuts in this process, to be sure. But the alternatives move very close, very quickly, to a cost-plus contract.

Neither of these alternatives made sense. The board saw no justification for waiting months while it prepared blueprints for a call for bids, trying in the meantime to mobilize a syndicate of contractors to submit responsible bids. The board not only recognized but welcomed its managerial responsibility and accountability as spelled out in the Act. It sought no escape hatch and wanted no predesigned alibi for failure. The board decided to create its own organization and hold itself responsible directly for construction. Thus the construction of dams and the development of detailed plans could go forward concurrently. Benefits from the finished structures would become available at an earlier date. Costs could be controlled. This original decision has never been changed. Twenty years later TVA thinks the plan was wise. Time and money have been saved, since its construction forces are able to take advantage of unusual conditions as they develop. There is no need to halt while expensive and time-consuming contractual changes are worked out.

By having direct control of its work, TVA is able to eliminate middleman costs for managerial services; accept its responsibilities in such matters as employee housing and general working conditions; meet across the table with its employees to work out problems which might otherwise delay the work or end in bitter disputes; and make economical, efficient, and full use of its trained construction crews and heavy-construction equipment from dam to dam.

The board met for the first time on June 16, 1933. On October 1, 1933, less than four months later, the building of Norris Dam was begun.

By the end of the first year an organization of ten thousand men and women had been assembled and was at work. Two dams had been started—the Norris Dam on the Clinch River near Knoxville and the Wheeler Dam on the main stem of the Tennessee above Wilson Dam at Muscle Shoals. Sites and foundations for additional dams were being explored. Engineering survey parties with rod, chain, and transit were running contours, later to show in the work of a mapping organization which has become one of the outstanding operations in the history of map-making.

The story of how TVA built its engineering design staff illustrates some of the problems it encountered in creating an organization committed by law to pioneer in engineering theory and make it work. These dams were to provide water storage for navigation and power and at the same time hold empty storage for flood control. The board was faced with the problem of finding engineers not only able to accept responsibility for the biggest construction job on earth at that time but willing to test their reputations on reconciling what many in their profession believed to be conflicting purposes.

To get construction under way at once, TVA turned to a pre-eminent design organization in the Bureau of Reclamation in Denver for help in designing the first projects.

While Norris and Wheeler were being built, it sent men around the country to find the engineering and architectural imagination and skill required to rebuild a whole river. Unhampered by restrictive civil service rules and stubbornly impervious to political and other pressures, it sought out candidates and screened and rescreened them to build its staff. Specialists in a variety of different engineering disciplines were selected and put to work, figuratively, around the same drawing board. Thus, when construction of the Pickwick Dam was ready to start in March, 1935, TVA's "E&C" forces—its engineering and construction people—had come into being. Location and general plans for the dam were decided by its water-control planning engineers; designs, drawings, and specifications were a TVA product; the field forces to build were TVA; and a TVA operating force was being mobilized to take over the finished structures.

There are many important measures of results. Reduced cost of design is one. Design costs for its first job—Pickwick Dam—were 5 per cent of the cost of the dam, a reasonable standard among private builders. The design costs for Douglas Dam, begun seven years and twelve dams later, were held to an incredible 1 per cent. Design costs today for TVA's giant, complex steam plants are approximately 2 per cent. And these structures not only serve well the purposes for which they were built; they fit the majesty of the landscape.

Merit and Efficiency versus Patronage

In 1933 unemployment, despair, a beaten pride, and disillusion created special problems of recruitment and selection of personnel. Dam construction started when pressure for relief work was high. In this prevailing mood it was realized that the desperate assertion of the right to work would make it difficult to insist upon competence. Unless a fair device could be found for the selection of skilled and unskilled workers, the insinuation of political patronage, goaded by the pressure of unemployed multitudes upon their congressmen and senators, would inevitably follow. For these reasons TVA devised a special method for the selection of its construction workers—a method to demonstrate right at the start that it intended to give life to Section 6 of its Act, the prohibition of political test or influence in TVA's employment. TVA conferred with the Civil Service Commission and obtained the able counsel of Dr. L. J. O'Rourke, then head of the Commission's research staff. From these consultations it was decided to hold examinations throughout the Tennessee Valley, from which a closed register of applicants would be established.

In the fall of 1933 two examinations were held in 138 centers, covering all Tennessee and parts of Kentucky, Virginia, North Carolina, Alabama, Georgia, and Mississippi. The examination was of a general type, to test ability to follow written and oral instructions. Admission to the examination was by card, issued to those whose applications met the requirement of residence within the Tennessee Valley. The application carried in the upper left-hand corner "Form 10 TVA." Of the tens of thousands of Form 10 applications freely distributed throughout the Valley, fifty thousand were filled out and returned, and almost thirty-nine thousand men ultimately took the examination.

The thousands of men from farms and cities, from mountain coves and cotton-gin towns, who assembled, pencil in hand, on those two December days of 1933 were probably unaware that they were making history in a method for the recruitment and selection of a labor force. Their presence in the post-office rooms, schoolhouses, and churches which served as examination centers was a public demonstration of a new approach to construction work. They had already passed, unknowingly, through several sifting screens. They were men who had decided to assemble for this strange kind of examination instead of relying on the assurance of harassed political captains that a job would be obtained for the party faithfuls without going through special procedures. They had shown their confidence in the probity of TVA by filling out Form 10 in spite of some scoffing at this fancy way of getting a job when, as the wise boys said, "everyone knows a letter from the congressman will be enough." For many thousands of men this was a gamble. They might lose, and those who relied on patronage might win. The men who appeared had been told that TVA was seeking to build a superior force to build dams, not just to lay bricks, to drive a truck, or to operate a jackhammer, but *to build dams*—dams to control floods, open up navigation, and produce power for homes, factories, and farms!

There was no need for a rank order in the register of those thirty-nine thousand men. To be sure, their individual achievement on the test was one of the factors considered in selection, as was intended, but the group as a whole had, in a very large sense, already "passed." The register thus established served all needs for skilled, semiskilled, and unskilled workmen through two years and the beginning of three dams—Norris, Wheeler, and Pickwick Landing.

But the Form 10 process did more than this. It laid the basis for public understanding throughout the Valley that TVA intended to be a different kind of public agency—an agency that did what it said it would do. "TVA Form 10" became a household phrase, a symbol of a search for skill and integrity in the employment and management of men. For when a man presented himself for employment at a personnel office on a construction job, he was asked, "Are you a Form 10 man?" If he was, he was eligible for further examination and employment. If not, his search for employment with the Authority was fruitless unless it was directed to something other than trades and labor services.

The effect of this process was shown when the next examination was held. This examination harvested ninety-eight thousand applications in three weeks from a smaller area within commuting distance of the sites for the next three dams. The word had gone around. So well had this process achieved its purpose that closed registers could later give way to open registers. The foundation for selection on merit had been laid.

The decision to build dams with its own construction forces and the decision to use systematic recruitment and employment procedures for skilled and unskilled workers, as well as for professional, clerical, and administrative applicants, were among the most important early managerial acts. They set in motion a chain of events and obligations which helped to build into a growing organization a respect and aspiration for merit, efficiency, and accountability for results. These were the important criteria that were to prevail throughout the progress of the work.

Union-Management Co-operation

As a direct employer TVA faced another important problem. In 1933 collective bargaining in the public service was little more than an academic question and was yet to be recognized by federal statute, even for private enterprise.

The collective-bargaining issue could have been evaded by electing to build dams by contract instead of by a force of its own employees. Recognition of the crucial nature of this problem and the opportunity to do something constructive about it influenced the board in its decision to assume the full responsibility of a direct employer.

Employees, construction supervisors, and labor leaders wanted to know what TVA proposed to do about unions, wages, grievances, and working conditions in general. Thus, it became necessary to develop a statement of policy that would make clear the principles and procedures which were to govern relationships between management and employees. After more than a year and a half of discussion, conference, and negotiation with groups of employees—organized and unorganized—and members of the staff, the board formally set forth its policies in 1935. Here they might have rejected collective bargaining and discouraged employees from joining unions; they could have emphasized the sovereignty of the government or argued long about the right to strike. But they left these more abstract questions to the future for test in specific cases.

The board's policy of 1935 recognized the right of employees to organize, to affiliate as they chose, to designate representatives, and to bargain collectively with the management. It established the machinery for handling grievances and the development of co-operative relationships with labor and employee organizations. This policy also established principles relating to employment standards—hours of work, compensation, training, promotion, and procedures for discharge.

Later these policies were incorporated with substantial revision into a signed general agreement[7] between TVA and the fifteen trades and labor unions of the American Federation of Labor on behalf of all trades and labor employees. The signed agreement recognizes the Tennessee Valley Trades and Labor Council as the negotiating agent for all matters within TVA affecting trades and labor employees. This council, formally recognized by the AF of L, was created by employees through their individual unions to co-ordinate and combine their representations to the management. The General Agreement establishes machinery for the settlement, by an impartial referee, of disputes not adjusted satisfactorily by the grievance procedure—a provision, incidentally, which has been invoked but twice in the last thirteen years.

Under the written agreements with the unions most of the problems that enter into the formulation of personnel policy have become the product of joint union-management committees. There is a joint wage conference in which wage rates are negotiated on a Valley-wide basis

7. *General Agreement between the Tennessee Valley Authority and the Tennessee Valley Trades and Labor Council, Negotiated August 6, 1940, Revised July 1, 1951, and Supplementary Schedules, Revised July 1, 1951* (Knoxville, 1951).

and a joint classification committee, both set up under the auspices of the council and the TVA management.

The agreement provides for a system of apprenticeship training in the skilled trades under the administration of a central joint apprenticeship council. This apprenticeship system has been invaluable—it has graduated nearly a thousand highly skilled journeymen and has produced many foremen, general foremen, and even construction superintendents from union ranks. Many began as unskilled young men, with little or no construction experience. They have become superior construction career men, whose pattern of study, training, and tests of performance and progress parallels the career standards of their professional colleagues. One man began as a laborer in 1936, trained as a steamfitter apprentice, and later became an assistant construction superintendent at TVA's largest steam plant. Another laborer, who helped to build Wheeler Dam in 1934, rose through training and promotion to become the project manager over all operations for the construction of one of the huge steam plants. And so the record goes in case after case. Here is a record of joint union-management co-operation in discovering and building competence; for many of these trained men have risen to the highest posts of construction responsibility and on all manner of private construction jobs in the area or are employed in responsible positions on the many huge national defense projects built in recent years.

These arrangements apply specifically to what are called trades and labor employees. They constitute a large proportion of TVA's forces. Union organizations among the so-called "white-collar" groups, who are referred to as "Salary Policy Employees," did not develop so rapidly as among trades and labor groups. It was several years before the salaried employees formed, and the management recognized for bargaining purposes, the Salary Policy Employee Panel. And, by 1950, articles of agreement were negotiated and signed.[8]

8. *Articles of Agreement between the Tennessee Valley Authority and the Salary Policy Employee Panel, Negotiated December 5, 1950, Revised May 1, 1952* (Knoxville, 1952).

In the long-evolving relationships with employees and their unions there have been difficulties and misunderstandings. But at no time have the arrangements agreed upon proved inadequate to resolve the crises common to large-scale construction and complicated operating requirements.

The capstone of these union-management arrangements is a system of joint co-operative union-management committees established by agreement to consider ways of improving job efficiency and reducing costs. These committees were contemplated in the earliest statement of board policy, in 1935, but they were not established until many years later. Delay in the establishment of these committees was deliberate. It was clear to both parties that it was useless to attempt to foster creative co-operation to improve efficiency until the basic procedures for handling problems of wages, hours, working conditions, grievances, and disputes had been established and tested by time and a practice of good faith.

In the last eleven years, thirty-eight union-management co-operative committees have been established. They have built an impressive record. More than fifty-five hundred proposals and ideas have been received, and 78 per cent of the ideas considered have been adopted. Almost half of the proposals concerned ways of doing the job better, quicker, cheaper, or easier. By this process TVA and the unions have tapped a veritable mine of knowledge, common sense, and ingenuity. Perhaps it is a new kind of jig to cut unit costs by speeding up some bending, grinding, or punching operation. Or it may be a way to build reusable cantilever concrete forms from used lumber and bolts that will save, as this idea did, $20,000 in the construction of two dams. One idea worked out a way to reschedule the operations of men and machines and produced a world's record for speed in tunnel work— 951 linear feet in three weeks' time! It may be an automatic float switch for a tank or an automatic time-clock switch to turn on an air compressor, as two recent ones were—each saved money for TVA. Many ideas proposed by employees eliminated the jobs of some employees. This process saves money, to be sure. But how different this is from the not uncommon atmosphere of a job where the boss "does the thinking around here" and the worker is expected to do only what he is told.

In the history of these committees there is one incident that reveals an unusual test of the fiber and purpose of all these relationships. It occurred to many that some system of recognition should be worked out for those employees whose proposals were used. Congress has established a money-award system for money-saving ideas, and many agencies are granting prizes of substantial amounts. After careful study of this plan by local committees and the central joint union-management committee, the idea of cash awards was rejected. The reason given was simple: the purpose of the joint committee was to build co-operation; individual awards would discourage it. Here is a type of responsibility that is priceless—a sense of the need for recognizing and encouraging co-operation among men.

By these and other means TVA was prepared for its contribution to the national defense in World War II. By 1943 it was building dams by assembly-line methods. At one time during the war twelve dams, as well as a steam plant and other facilities, were under construction. At the peak of the war its forces numbered some forty-two thousand men and women, most of them in construction. By 1946, with the war over, these forces were reduced to eleven thousand. This was not as a result of an economy drive imposed from the outside but in the normal course of the board's adherence to the tests of accountability.

It is not important here to recite the story of each of the twenty dams TVA has built. There are two recitals, however, which illustrate what is meant by the discipline of full accountability for results. One is the story of Douglas Dam, built during the war, a saga of great importance in the history of rebuilding the river. The other is a chapter still being written; it is the story of the Shawnee Steam Plant now under construction and in partial operation near Paducah, Kentucky, to supply a major part of the electric power required for the Atomic Energy Commission's new facilities there.

The Douglas Dam Story

In the spring of 1941, months before Pearl Harbor, the Office of Production Management, predecessor to the War Production Board, foresaw the need for at least 100,000 kilowatts of additional power in the Tennessee Valley to expand aluminum production for more bombers. The Authority was therefore asked to recommend a program to build in the shortest time possible, but by the winter of 1943 at the latest, at least 100,000 kilowatts of power.

There were several alternatives, but by the time the OPM reached its decision only one of the several projects in the planning stage could be guaranteed to meet the requirements of the OPM's request. Only Douglas Dam, in the judgment of TVA's engineers, would produce the power in the time required. The board accepted the recommendation of its engineers, and the President, with the indorsement of the OPM, recommended appropriations by Congress to begin construction of the dam at once. This was in the late summer of 1941, some five months before Pearl Harbor.

As soon as this request reached Congress, with the recommendation of the President, the Office of Production Management, and the Tennessee Valley Authority, powerful interests whose landholdings and business would be affected by the flooding of the bottom lands along the French Broad River behind the Douglas Dam site raised strenuous protest. They sought and gained the help of powerful men on the Appropriations Committee. A major battle ensued. Funds would be made available to build dams, it was said, *but not this dam.* This dam, Douglas Dam, the Authority was told, was not politically possible. Senators became engineers. They urged TVA's engineers to become politicians. They called attention to four other dams which might be built instead of Douglas. Two of them were on another tributary of the Tennessee and were included in the catalogue of future projects. Two more were on a neighboring river over which the Army Corps of Engineers has jurisdiction.

Admittedly, the suggested alternatives would arouse less opposition and would not conflict with the business interests prominent in the Douglas Dam reservoir. But the four dams would take longer to build and would not meet the power requirements.[9] Stream-flow records for the two dams proposed as an alternative gave no assurance that the reservoirs would fill in one season, and together they would not provide the power required. The Douglas project was the only one which would provide 100,000 kilowatts of power capacity in the time specified by the war production agency.

The board, therefore, declined to withdraw or change the recommendations of its engineers, but Congress elected to follow the contrary judgment and in the fall of 1941 directed TVA to begin construction of the alternative projects. There were counselors aplenty who pointed out that the Authority was stubborn and foolish in continuing to push the claims of the Douglas site. There were many friends who warned of the price that would have to be paid for intransigence. The board stood firm. The facts of engineering could not be denied. A month after Pearl Harbor, opposition was withdrawn and work began.

There were penalties to pay. One was a construction hazard. Because of the delay, instead of beginning in the dry fall season as planned, construction on the dam had to start in early winter, with flood flows jeopardizing the progress of the work and increasing its cost. By this time it was January, 1942, and the tough sixteen-month schedule assumed in the promises to the War Production Board had to be shortened. The dam had to be finished before the rains of the next winter. There is no need here to go into the details of superhuman effort, the extraordinary mobilization of men, materials, and ideas and leadership that went into the construction of Douglas Dam under the most adverse circumstances. But let me report with pride that on February 19, 1943, twelve months and sixteen days from the time con-

9. The two Holston dams were authorized in place of Douglas when Douglas was first turned down by Congress. They were later stopped by the War Production Board because it was clear, as TVA had pointed out, that their completion was not possible within the time required for additional increments of power in the national war production program. Both dams were completed after the war.

struction started, the gates closed and water began backing up behind Douglas Dam.

The following month a ceremony was held, and a construction worker who had not been absent a single day was selected by the men to throw the switch that started the generators to work. TVA had kept its commitment. The power required to provide the aluminum for the goal of fifty thousand planes a year was on the line. Bombers that later prepared the Normandy beaches for D-Day, to begin the Great Crusade in Europe, took their place on time because TVA's engineers, workers, and managers had turned in a record-breaking performance. TVA, standing behind the integrity of its engineers and the dedicated skill of its working forces, had delivered. A new world's record for speed of large-dam construction had been made.

But this was not to be the end of the story of Douglas Dam. The delay was paid for in extra effort. There were other payments. Before construction of Douglas Dam was two months under way, the consequences of TVA's stubbornness began to appear. First, a bill was introduced which would have amended the Act by stripping the Authority of the use of its revenues in the conduct of its power business and in other ways restrict its work. The bill was defeated. Another measure was pressed which would have made every employee receiving a salary of $4,500 or more a year subject to confirmation by the Senate. It might, if it had been adopted, have been effective in turning engineers into politicians. But it was not adopted. And the reason why this and other amendments which would have stripped the Authority of its competence and bartered away its integrity failed to pass was because the people of the region and the majority of its representatives in the Congress rose in protest. In the end those efforts to put TVA in politics, to divest it of management responsibilities, and to dishonor its objectives became an occasion for public understanding and support. The understanding of the people developed in those tumultuous years is TVA's stoutest bulwark now.

This is what accountability finally means: taking whatever penalties accrue. It is a severe discipline. It is not unknown for the recommendations of technicians and engineers to be forsaken by top administrators when the going gets tough. It is not unprecedented for agencies to trim their sails according to political winds or for the heavy hands of powerful individuals to get results. But administrators pay a high price for yielding to pressures that break into the circle of their responsibility. They are, in effect, making political decisions under the guise of administrative, engineering, or other professional responsibilities.

Now TVA always recognized that Congress had the responsibility for deciding whether or not Douglas Dam should be built. Its responsibility was to explain and defend its best recommendation as a solution to the problem set forth by the Executive. It was quite ready to be held accountable for its recommendations; it was not willing to adopt a political judgment as its own and present it under the guise of an engineering or administrative recommendation.

If TVA had yielded in the Douglas Dam controversy, it would have lost its status as an engineering organization; it would have demonstrated that its recommendations could not be trusted. I can say that, if the board had failed to stand by the recommendations of its engineers for this specific program under these special circumstances, it could never again have trusted its engineers completely. Those engineers would have recognized that the Authority was not prepared to stand back of the integrity of the organization. The engineers would have been encouraged to trim and hedge, trying to predict the political acceptability of the various compromises they might devise. Under such circumstances the board could never have been sure whether it was receiving an engineering judgment from professional engineers or a political judgment from amateur politicians. Despite the heavy penalty of controversy as a consequence of its decision, the organization and the region came through the Douglas Dam affair strengthened by the process. And in the years since Douglas Dam, whenever there has been a temptation within TVA to subvert the integrity of its judgments to avoid political consequences or personal abuse, the phrase, "Remember Douglas Dam," has been enough to fortify its courage and bring its thinking back onto the track.

There is more, much more, to the significance of the Douglas Dam chapter in the history of TVA. This feat of construction could not have been accomplished had it not been for the years of preparation, practice, training, and achievement that preceded it. Had the board been in the practice of letting dams to contract, it would not even have been possible for it to have recommended the project to the President or to have met the critically shortened schedule. If the job had been let to contract, the news that the bill was signed and had become a law would have been the signal for contracts to be signed, for lawyers to get together for final agreements on details of risks and profits. Weeks or months later construction would have begun. As it was, this is what happened: The moment the bill was signed by the President, the chief clerk at the White House called the Washington office of TVA. The chief engineer in Knoxville was at his telephone, with a cleared line waiting for the news. His gesture to his assistant started bulldozers, tractors, and giant dirt-moving equipment on the site. Dormitories and shop buildings from the nearest construction project began the trek to Douglas. In anticipation the top organization for the Douglas Dam project had been hand-picked from twelve other projects under construction. They had been carefully trained and briefed weeks before the appropriation bill was signed. For the skilled labor force lead men had been selected, around whom new crews were built from available registers with great speed.

Design drawings, orders for equipment, and instructions and assignments had been prepared weeks in advance and were on the desks ready for execution by appropriate officers throughout the organization. Not one moment was wasted. When the word to begin came through, the whole organization started. Land-buyers took up their work, road and bridge relocations were begun, generators and turbines placed on order. The skill and organization built up through the 1930's, and tried by the test of performance, paid off as a wartime dividend. TVA did not know then that the 100,000 kilowatts of power to be produced by Douglas Dam from the flow of the French Broad River were needed to serve a load even more urgent than the aluminum requirements for the expanded bomber program. It was only later that it realized that some of the power from Douglas Dam was required for the atomic-bomb project at Oak Ridge.

Accountability for results exerts its severe discipline in many ways. In a sense a government agency, in seeking appropriations justified by what the experts call a "performance budget" is negotiating a contract with Congress, the representative of the taxpayer. When TVA asks for money to begin a new project, it gives an engineering estimate of the total cost of that project. A measure of its response to the theory of accountability may be found in this fact: In these twenty years the actual cost for twenty dams and three major steam plants now completed is within seven-tenths of 1 per cent of the estimates made at the time the funds for the projects were requested of Congress. This applies to a total of $847 million covering thousands upon thousands of separate engineering estimates that are summarized by a single figure for each dam—a figure covering the bits and pieces, the large generators, the land to be purchased, and the man-hours to be used.

Consider, if you will, what this record might have been had TVA been required to have its dams planned and located by one agency, designed by another, and the actual work performed by contractors. What if the land had had to be purchased by a different bureau, and contract negotiations and litigation handled by a separate government department, with the employees recruited and certified by a still different agency, and procurement of materials and equipment in the hands of someone else. Under these circumstances Douglas Dam could not have been built in record-breaking time, if at all. Under these circumstances it is probable that Douglas Dam would not have been recommended in the face of promised political furor. When the board of TVA told the war production agency, the President, and Congress that it could build Douglas Dam by the deadline required, it was backed by knowledge that there was within its own hands the managerial organization to deliver what it promised. Had this project been approached in piecemeal fashion with responsibilities scattered among other agencies whose special duties to this project would be but a part of larger national programs, there could have been a dozen built-in alibis for its failure to finish Douglas Dam on time. Here in this recital we have an illustration of what President Theodore Roosevelt said in 1908: "We shall not succeed . . . until the responsibility for administering the policy and executing and extending the plan is definitely laid on one man or group of men who can be held accountable."[10]

Measuring up to a high standard of accountability brings rewards beyond calculation. If you should visit TVA and talk with its employees, meet its project managers, and walk around on its construction jobs, perhaps you, like others, would be impressed with what you see and what you hear. The story of Douglas Dam is in part an explanation of the prevailing spirit. Money will not buy it; high salaries cannot command it. Integrity and a practice of high expectations must be among the ingredients to produce that result.

The story of how the Tennessee River was rebuilt certainly does not support the too-often-accepted myth that everything of government is inefficient, corrupt, and wasteful. What has been described would find many parallels among many government agencies within the states, within the cities, within the federal government. But these stories of achievement are seldom heard against the din of criticism.

Shawnee and Atomic Energy

I move now to another chapter in the history of TVA—the story of the Shawnee Steam Plant at Paducah, Kentucky. Except for the Authority's Kingston Steam Plant, the Shawnee Steam Plant will be the biggest in the world. During each twenty-four-hour day its ten giant units will consume nearly 14,000 tons of coal and can return each day to the alchemy of national defense and the growth of the nation more than half as much electric energy as is used in Chicago. The Shawnee

10. *Preliminary Report of the Inland Waterways Commission*, p. 5.

Steam Plant is but one of seven under construction, but it has a special history.

In the fall of 1950 the Atomic Energy Commission asked TVA, on very short notice, to develop a proposal to supply 1,000,000 kilowatts of power for a new gaseous diffusion plant the AEC was to build at Paducah. A plan was submitted, and the Atomic Energy Commission accepted it early in November, 1950. Shortly thereafter, the Commission's representatives, followed by those of the Authority, appeared before the House Committee on Appropriations to support a request for funds. Later in December, before the committee had acted upon this request, the Atomic Energy Commission announced that it had accepted the proposal of a newly formed private utility company to supply half the required power for the AEC plant. The new company had been formed at the behest of a member of the Atomic Energy Commission, as subsequently explained by the Commissioner in a very illuminating speech.

TVA did not object to this sudden reversal of the Atomic Energy Commission's position and appeared again before the House Committee on Appropriations with an appropriation request, revised in accord with AEC's decision, to supply, not all, but half of the power supply for the Paducah plant. The Atomic Energy Commission entered into a contract with the newly formed Electric Energy, Incorporated, to supply the other half. In both cases the construction of new steam plants was called for.

The announcement that the power supply for the AEC Paducah plant was to be divided between TVA and Electric Energy, Inc., was hailed by critics of the Authority as a contest between public and private enterprise, giving rise to such statements as the following: "Accordingly many companies pooled their ideas and their resources . . . for the expressed purpose of demonstrating to the government that private enterprise could do the job much better for half the cost."[11]

There was some reason for the optimism thus expressed by these

11. Editorial, "A Real Test," *Cairo* (Ill.) *Evening Citizen*, February 24, 1953.

sideline critics, for, when the construction of the two plants was started, the first unit of the private company's steam plant at Joppa, Illinois, was scheduled for initial operation three months ahead of TVA's first unit. The schedules were set by agreement between AEC, national defense agencies in charge of allocating materials, TVA, and Electric Energy, Inc. Priorities on steel, copper, aluminum, and shop space for the manufacturing of turbogenerators were granted to the Joppa contractors on that basis. If this was to be a race, it was a handicap run by agreement.

For many months the champions of private enterprise continued to point a gleeful finger at this rigged contest between the private power company and TVA. Trade journals and some of the daily press heralded this "race" being run on opposite sides of the beautiful Ohio. After a while the cries of the professional spectators died down. The reason was easy to discern. It began to be apparent that the wrong horse was coming in ahead.

Both TVA and Electric Energy, Inc., suffered from delayed deliveries from equipment manufacturers. Both encountered labor difficulties. Both projects missed the completion dates originally scheduled. But on April 9, 1953, approximately two years and three months from the time construction was started, the first unit at TVA's Shawnee plant was placed in commercial operation, while the Joppa smokestacks across the river were still clean and cold. The second Shawnee unit went into operation on June 21, 1953. Still no smoke from Joppa. Several weeks later the first unit in the Joppa plant was placed in operation. The third Shawnee unit was placed in operation in October; its fourth unit on January 8, 1954. By this time two of the four Joppa units were running. Thus the original requirements promised the AEC by TVA were completed when the Joppa plant still had a long way to go. So much for the much-publicized race between private and public enterprise.

But there is more to the story. Judging by figures filed with the Securities and Exchange Commission, the private company's Joppa plant will be substantially more expensive per unit of capacity than the Shawnee plant, in contrast with the original estimates by which the private company's contract was obtained from the AEC.

These figures show that the estimated cost of the private company's Joppa Steam Plant of four original units has increased some 45 per cent—from $81 million in May, 1951, to $118 million in June, 1953. The costs per kilowatt of capacity have increased over their original estimate of $126 to $184. Two more units at the Joppa plant being added to supply a smaller portion of AEC's expanded Paducah facilities show estimates even higher—$198 per kilowatt. The taxpayers bought this record, and they will have to pay for it; the private companies lose nothing, because these increased costs are paid by the AEC.

In comparison, the Shawnee plant of four units was originally estimated to cost $147.50 per kilowatt. TVA's actual cost experience to date, while building under the same physical conditions as the Joppa plant, shows that the total ten-unit Shawnee plant capable of producing 1,500,000 kilowatts will be completed at a capital cost well within its estimates.

Let me add a few footnotes and observations bearing upon the significance of the Shawnee-Joppa story in TVA's record in these last twenty years.

Early in June, 1953, before it had its first generating unit in operation, Electric Energy, Inc., was given the Charles A. Coffin Award in a ceremony at the annual convention of the Edison Electric Institute. The *Institute Bulletin* reported the award as the "electric industry's highest honor." The citation commended Electric Energy, Inc., for "its superb example of competitive enterprise."[12]

On July 31, 1953, Electric Energy, Inc., announced it had canceled its contract with Ebasco Services, general contractor for the plant, "in order to permit reorganization of the construction project so that the station can be completed on a more efficient and economical basis." The reorganization was necessary, according to the president

12. "Electric Energy, Inc., Wins Charles A. Coffin Award," *Edison Electric Institute Bulletin*, XXI (July, 1953), 234.

of Electric Energy, Inc., as reported in the *Paducah Sun-Democrat*, "be-cause of the lack of productivity and consequent increased costs characterizing the work so far."[13]

The *Wall Street Journal* reported that "construction progress at the big power plant has been marked by successively rising cost estimates, blamed by Ebasco on the labor situation."[14] However, as the *Paducah Sun-Democrat* pointed out: "Shawnee Steam Plant is being built with the same kind of union labor that is building Joppa's plant."[15]

The comment of the *Paducah Sun-Democrat* was correct but incom-plete. The Shawnee plant was being built with the same kind of union labor that was building the Joppa plant, but the men on the job were working for TVA. For as one reporter, who surveyed the situa-tion with great care, stated, "For some reason the men who work for TVA have faith in it." The Authority does not consider its Shawnee record the brightest in its catalogue of construction projects. It has built dams and steam plants on better schedule, with fewer difficulties, and at lower cost. But others invited the comparison between Shawnee and Joppa, and it is that record I recite.

There have been work stoppages on the Shawnee plant, but not as many as they have had across the river at Joppa. The labor forces have been drawn from the same areas; the wage rates are about the same; and both are building steam plants. The design and manufacture of boilers, turbines, and generators; the fabrication of steel; the erection of steel on the site; the operation of excavating equipment; and the placing of concrete are much the same types of operations whether at Shawnee or at Joppa. Both projects depended upon private manu-facturers for boilers, turbogenerators, and the thousands of items of equipment which enter the maze of arrangements in a modern steam plant. Why, then, was TVA able to move out in front and keep its

13. *Paducah* (Ky.) *Sun-Democrat*, July 31, 1953.

14. *Wall Street Journal*, August 3, 1953.

15. *Paducah* (Ky.) *Sun-Democrat*, April 8, 1953.

costs within its estimates as compared with the job across the river? Its history provides the answer: the twenty-year record of an organization skilled in management of men and materials and pledged to a practice of performance and accountability time after time.

The Shawnee story adds another chapter to record the achievement by a government agency in conflict with the myth that enterprise and good management are the exclusive possessions of private organizations. The men who promoted the arrangement perhaps believed that the requirements of national security, the need for certainty of power supply when the Paducah AEC plant was ready, called for participation by private companies to hedge the possible failure of TVA. Perhaps there was not time enough for them to examine the facts of the record of the past. Perhaps the American taxpayer could have been saved the burden of the increased cost to the government of this electrical energy had those who made the decision questioned the common myth, too often honored, which holds that government can never do a job as well or as economically as can private contractors.

Had the facts been examined, they would have found a record of performance reassuring both as to TVA's ability to meet deadlines and as to the reliability of its estimates of cost. They would have found a history of hundreds of millions of man-hours with a safety record better than private industry averages for comparable types of work. They would have found an engineering organization designing steam plants which were producing electricity more economically and with more efficient use of fuel than most—a significant point, indeed, when one realizes that in two or three years TVA will be burning some 18,000,000 tons of coal per year. Above all, they would have found an organization of construction workers still as unafraid to tackle the biggest construction job on earth as in those first days— workers who override emergencies. If they do not have what they need, they invent a substitute way on the spot, and the job moves ahead.

If this story has a moral, perhaps this is it: Enterprise is where you find it.

Conclusion

The record of TVA's men and management in rebuilding a river will never completely be told, but the results of this achievement can be put into words. Let me summarize them briefly: The flow of water in the river is now controlled. The devastation of floods has been reduced to manageable proportions in the Tennessee Valley. Already the savings from the control of floods at one city alone—Chattanooga—have totaled more than one-fourth of the flood-control investment in the entire river system. Other regions benefit, too, for the dams reduce the crests of floods on the lower Ohio and the Mississippi by the 2 or 3 feet which make the difference between safety and community disaster. That much is done. Those benefits will grow while the expenditures diminish.

Navigation locks in the dams and a stable channel have made possible a growing commerce on the river. More commerce means more jobs, new markets, and greater economic opportunities for the people of this region and the Mississippi Valley. In 1933, the year TVA began its work, about 33,000,000 ton-miles of freight were shipped on the river, for the most part cargo of low value. Last year the rebuilt river carried a billion ton-miles, much of it of high-value products— petroleum, automobiles, grain, coal, and fertilizer. More commerce will be carried every year. Greater savings to shippers and to consumers will be added each year.

The dams are here to stay. Concrete, earth fill, and rock make them a permanent part of a landscape more hospitable to human endeavor than it used to be. New kinds of enterprises find a climate for growth in this area because the river is controlled. For the dams that hold back the waters in time of floods, and fill the channel in time of drought, create beautiful lakes, a setting for the third largest and newest business of the area—recreation. And, for good measure, these majestic dams and modern steam plants provide the electric power which has changed the lives of people on their farms, in their homes, and in new industries throughout the region.

This is a record of men at work. There was no Aladdin's lamp to rub. Geologists and engineers, cartographers and surveyors, accountants and land-buyers, draftsmen and doctors, union leaders, ironworkers, carpenters—the hard-hat legions of TVA's construction crews—men of more than a score of professions and hundreds of occupations, have dedicated their talents to this job. In these twenty years scores of thousands of American citizens have worked at one time or another up and down the Tennessee Valley, driving machines and moving mountains to build these great projects to serve mankind. Not, like the pyramids, as monuments to men of lofty station. Not for the glory of the designers, engineers, or workmen. Not for the profit of a few. The purpose of the structures stands inscribed upon each one: "Built for the People of the United States."

III. TVA and the People

The Tennessee Valley Authority is many things to many people. The farmer who advertises a farm for sale in the local paper summarizes a whole chapter of change in two words: "Has TVA." The prospective buyer knows the words mean low-cost electricity for bright light in the house and barn—at dusk and before sunup for choretime. He knows it means a chance to use water pumps, milking machines, chicken brooders, power tools—devices to spare his back and increase his income. His wife knows it can mean an electric washing machine, a refrigerator, possibly a gleaming white kitchen and television.

To many thousands of young men and women the TVA means a wider range of choice in finding a job. Even in the boom year of 1929 many people had to choose between two sharp alternatives: staying on the farm where their labor was not rewarded or making the long and costly trek to Detroit, Chicago, or Cleveland to look for a factory job. Today, the new factories in Decatur, Alabama, or Calvert City, Kentucky, or Calhoun, Tennessee—among many others—add to the freedom of choice. Many thousands can now work in a factory near home and do some farming too.

Or perhaps the future beckons with a job or a small-business opportunity in the spreading network of enterprise that caters to the fishermen and tourists now attracted in tens of thousands to the beauty and pleasure available in the new lakes of the South. TVA is many things to many people, indeed.

Much has happened to the people of the Tennessee Valley in the last twenty years. But let no one nurse the notion that the Authority has wrought the change singlehandedly. The great changes in the Valley have come through a far-reaching coalition of effort, sparked at the center by a new kind of administrative arrangement—the TVA—through which agencies of the states, local communities, and thousands of citizens have joined to put the resources of the region to work in producing more income for more people. These many agencies and individuals have agreed generally that knowledge about the natural and human resources of the region can be a guide to intelligent decisions that promise a better future in the place they prefer to live.

Should farming depend primarily upon row crops—corn, cotton, and tobacco—exposing soil and people more inevitably to the ravages and risks of weather and the erratic rewards of distant markets? Or should—in fact, can—the fertility of the soil be restored to support diversified, grassland, livestock farming with reduced risk from the failure of a single crop? Must rough lumber from this last remaining great hardwood area of the nation be shipped to distant processing centers for other wage-earners and businessmen to extract the lion's share of the new wealth in the finished product, or can factories be established near by to create and retain a greater purchasing power at home? Can the region develop more places for more people to work as a new kind of farming and labor-saving electricity call for fewer hands upon the land? These are some of the questions the people of the Valley have been pondering and answering for themselves.

Much has been accomplished by the people of the Tennessee Valley in the last twenty years. In the 201 counties which comprise the Valley and the larger area reached by TVA electricity there are almost six million people. In 1929 the same area had a million fewer residents. And, while population increased, the income of the people increased at a greater pace than for the nation as a whole. In 1929 the average per capita income of the people of the region was 44 per cent of the national average; in 1952 it had risen to 61 per cent of the national average. Improved farming systems and a shift from agriculture to industry are the central themes of this revolutionary change.

Industry has expanded more rapidly in the Tennessee Valley region than in the Southeast or in the nation as a whole. This is true whether measured by source of income or by kind of employment. The Valley twenty years ago was primarily an agricultural region with few opportunities for industrial employment. Farms were small and farm families were large, so that many individuals who depended upon the land for a living were "underemployed." Aside from a large aluminum plant and a number of iron foundries, industry in the Valley was heavily concentrated in textiles and lumber, which paid low wages. When the 1929 depression struck the Valley, the ranks of the unemployed were quickly swelled by the large numbers who lost their jobs in Detroit and other northern centers and came home to look for food and shelter.

In the years since that dark day—darker in the Tennessee Valley than many now care to recall—the region has made long strides toward a better balance between agriculture and industry. With it have come arrangements for more efficient use of the region's resources, greater production, higher incomes, and a wider range of personal choice for farmers, businessmen, and wage-earners.

Here are some figures: In 1929 many more people lived in rural areas. Agriculture was the predominant way of life for 870,000, while 627,000 made their living in nonagricultural occupations. By 1952 the rearrangement the people had wrought was recorded in these figures: the number engaged in agriculture had decreased to 537,000, while other pursuits claimed 1,197,000. The increase in nonagricultural employment has behind it a story of industrial expansion, new factories, and a growth in general business—trade, service, finance, transportation, and construction.

Some of the details may interest those who want to probe the multiple cause-and-effect arrangements which spell dynamic economic development. I invite a quick review of these details because of the thousands of individual decisions they imply—decisions by people of the Valley and many, many people in other parts of the country whose energies, ideas, and private dollars went into these new opportunities and who are reaping a benefit in private profit.

From 1929 to 1952 the number of persons engaged in manufacturing in the 201 counties in the region of TVA electricity increased from

222,000 to 417,000.[1] Those in trades and services increased from 298,000 to 497,000. This category includes a doubling in trade and finance. While these increases in the variety and number of opportunities were taking place, the numbers in agriculture and mining dropped.

These changes show even more dramatically when recorded for source of income. In 1929 some 23 per cent of the region's income came from agriculture; manufacturing accounted for only 15 per cent. By 1952 this relationship had been reversed: 21 per cent came from manufacturing, and 13 per cent from agriculture.

And most significant: the high-wage industries—chemicals, for example—show a more rapid growth than the low-wage industries. By 1947 the chemical industry, a large user of electricity, employed 13 per cent of all factory workers in the region. Besides the atomic-energy operations at Oak Ridge, this expansion has come in the manufacturing and processing of rayon, nylon, and other synthetic fibers and in the production of phosphorus, alkalies, chlorine, plastics, drugs, fertilizers, and gum and wood chemicals.

The majority of the new industries of the area process native raw materials. They are widely distributed throughout the region. In 1949 a study of the new pattern of industrial development showed that one-third of the new plants are located in cities of more than 100,000—the few larger cities of the region. But more than one-third of the new manufacturing enterprises are in towns of less than 5,000 people, where the community reaches quickly into the surrounding rural neighborhoods to enlist the energies of the partially employed people who live on the land.

Forests, Industry, and Jobs

The new paper mill built on the banks of the Hiwassee River in southeastern Tennessee is an illuminating example of a private industrial concern that found the Valley ripe for the opportunity its manage-

1. All employment and income figures in this chapter are based upon special tabulations of national and state estimates by the United States Department of Commerce, applied to the area by the TVA Division of Regional Studies.

ment and money sought. The opportunity was made possible by the integrated development of the natural resources of a river valley and the initiative and decisions of many people.

The New York Times for October 10, 1954, reported the event in this way:

BRITONS DEDICATE
BIG MILL IN SOUTH

60-Million Newsprint Plant
'Sold Out' through 1969
—Queen Sends Greeting

Calhoun, Tenn., Oct. 9—The Bowaters Southern Paper Corporation dedicated its $60,000,000 newsprint mill here today in ceremonies attended by more than 450 newspaper publishers, paper industry representatives, state officials and other persons.

The mill is the largest of its kind to be built in the United States in more than a quarter-century, and the first American mill of the British-owned Bowater organization, a leading world producer.

The plant, whose main buildings extend 400 yards—the length of four football fields—began shipping newsprint last July to scores of Southern newspapers. It is producing at the annual rate of 130,000 tons, but this is scheduled to be increased to 150,000 by next summer. The company has announced plans to double the present capacity eventually.

. . . .

The newsprint mill is the third and largest built in the South.[2]

Calhoun is not a large town. As you swing over and down the ridge just before you cross the bridge that spans the Hiwassee as it flows on its way to join the Tennessee River, the newspaper mill spreads out before you. Calhoun is up the hill beyond the river. Automobiles, old and new, fill the ample parking lots of the Bowaters area. At shift time they leave to make way for others bringing the men who take the next shift. They come from farms and towns in and around the Chestuee Creek watershed—a tributary of the Hiwassee—of which you will read more in the chapter on "TVA and the States." Some of the same

2. Sec. L, p. 74.

men whose farms are in the timberlands whence the pulpwood comes will learn to tend the complicated machines that process the logs into pulp and paper—the very same paper they read at home to follow the news of the day.

The paper mill, already in production, will employ eight hundred people at the plant and provide work for several hundred more to supply pulpwood from the forests and woodlands. The plant operation, as now planned, will have an annual pay roll of $3,500,000. It will consume about a thousand cords of pine every day from a forest area extending over a radius of three hundred miles. This market will provide a yearly income of several million dollars for woodlot farmers and large forest-owners—the timber-growers of the region. The company has undertaken a reforestation program in which it intends to plant and manage on a sustained basis some five million pine seedlings a year on many thousands of acres of its own land. The company is supplementing state and county programs for forest-fire protection. Its policy is to encourage private landowners also to grow trees as a crop for pulpwood to supply the market created by the newsprint mill.

Behind the story of this new plant is a long record of study and research and hundreds of practical demonstrations in improved timber practices carried on by private landowners with the help of the TVA and state forestry experts. And underlying the careful work in forest conservation, the construction of dams to supply power, navigation, and flood control played a crucial part in making the Calhoun mill a reality.

When TVA began its work, the nature and extent of the forest resources in the Tennessee Valley were known only in the most general terms. Anyone traveling through the Valley could see that the forests and woodlands had been seriously depleted. Many areas of eroding agricultural land needed to be reclaimed through reforestation for watershed protection. These conditions were matters of general knowledge, but precise information was lacking. In 1939, therefore, the Authority started to make a detailed inventory of forest resources to determine the location, extent, and character of timber available in the region and to survey wood use by industries and by domestic users. In addition, the pattern of ownership of the forest lands and of the transportation arrangements for forest products was discovered and described. Forest taxation policies were examined to see what effect they might have upon the management of timberlands. These studies made it possible to make estimates of the wood-consumption requirements of the Valley and of the marketing areas near by.

By the time these investigations were completed, the very broad development of the pulp and paper industry in the Deep South was shaping up. The Tennessee Valley figured in this early interest, even though it was on the fringe of the southern pine area. Information on forest resources, power supplies and rates, water supplies and chemical analyses of water, tax rates, and labor and labor rates was being requested by consulting engineers, industrial agents of railroads, chambers of commerce, and others. TVA was prepared with factual answers on which businessmen, bankers, and engineers could base their decisions.

One of the many inquiries came from the Bowater Paper Company, Inc., the sales organization in the United States for the parent-company in London, England, a firm with pulp and paper manufacturing facilities in England, Sweden, Norway, and Newfoundland. Bowater was investigating possible sites for a newsprint mill in the South.

In 1944 a group of Bowater representatives got in touch with the Tennessee Valley Authority. Some southern newspaper publishers, they had learned, thought that such a mill would provide an appropriate use of the Valley's natural resources and at the same time meet the pressing need of southern newspapers for newsprint. Facts about the Valley were put into their hands. No more was heard until 1951, but in the meantime Bowater had surveyed some thirty-three areas, had analyzed the specific sites carefully spotted by TVA's studies, and had narrowed its selection to three possible sites in the South. By 1951 the company's plans had reached the point where the availability of electric power was an urgent consideration. The Authority assured the company that power would be available.

Bowater then proceeded to examine the forest resource in further detail. TVA, in the meantime, had made additional studies of the timber resources of the Valley. Bowater's foresters were impressed with the basic changes that had taken place in the steady development of the region. The program of encouraging replanting and reforestation on private lands was beginning to show results. Foresters were able to point to new stands of pine trees planted in the late 1930's to heal eroded slopes; now they grew in closed ranks ready for thinning. But owners needed a market for the small-growth timber which would be removed in the thinning process, or the pay-off for the investment would be too long deferred. A newsprint mill could be such a market.

Bowater became more interested in a Tennessee River site for its plant. Many more studies, investigations, and discussions followed. TVA provided information on the availability of timber from public lands adjacent to the reservoirs behind the dams and on problems of stream sanitation and the standards of pollution control established by the states of Tennessee and Alabama. The impact of a new, large industry on the immediate community in which it might locate was explored. Transportation problems were taken up with the Authority's navigation specialists. The effect of flood heights and the regulation of reservoirs on various possible sites was examined with facts readily at hand from the carefully kept records of the engineers.

Finally came the critical question that had to be answered with fact and careful estimate before a decision on a Valley plant site could be made. Would the forest resources of the Valley be sufficient to supply the large quantities of pulpwood this plant would require? The careful inventory of forest resources paid off with an affirmative answer— Bowaters Southern Paper Corporation began to build the plant.

The new paper mill is located on land which, without dams, would be subject to frequent floods. Much of its raw material arrives over a waterway made possible by the new system of dams. TVA electricity is the company's prime source of power; the small plant the company has built to supply steam used in the papermaking process is to be tied in with the larger power system, and its surplus capacity will be available to the Authority.

An additional market for forest products provides a new incentive for farmers and forest-owners to replant many acres in profitable pine. The temperate climate with its long growing season helps to produce a marketable pine tree in less time than it takes in the North Woods. And a good market for the fast-growing pine trees adds a powerful stimulus for more effective prevention and control of forest fires. Better care of forests helps to check soil erosion, and the water from heavy rains lingers longer on the land, reducing runoff and the harmful effects of small floods.

Mr. Garrison Siskin, president of Siskin Steel and Supply Company of Chattanooga, summarized the importance of these developments in a recent article in the *Yale Scientific Magazine.* "Bowaters' coming into this southern valley," he wrote, "is one more instance of how private enterprise is taking over the job of using profitably and wisely great natural resources which, if left undeveloped, would remain wastefully idle."[3]

Calhoun, Tennessee, and London, England, are tied together by a faster growth and a better harvest of trees, an enterprise that brings farms, woodlands, and the news presses of a new Southland into partnership with the formula of soil, sun, water, and human energy—for "the economic and social well-being of the people living in said river basin."[4] And few will contend that the benefits will stop at the basin's edge.

I wish there were space to call the roll of cities, towns, and just places where a burgeoning private enterprise is changing the landscape, creating new centers of work and production in the Tennessee Valley, and closing the gap in a once costly cycle of lost or idle resources—natural and human. Calhoun is but one example.

3. "Steel and Industry in the South," *Yale Scientific Magazine,* XXVIII (May, 1954), 11.

4. Act of May 18, 1933, Sec. 23 (48 Stat. 69).

A Dream That Came True

Calvert City in western Kentucky is another. This little community is within sight of the Tennessee River, not far from its junction with the Ohio at Paducah. Not long ago, before TVA built the Kentucky Dam near by, Calvert City was a village of three hundred people. Today, it is a busy place of a thousand, with the difficult job ahead of accommodating ten thousand people by 1960. A new multibillion-dollar industrial nucleus of chemical plants is now operating and building there.

Among its townsmen twenty years ago there was at least one who dreamed of the day when abundant electricity at low cost, produced from a dam sometime certain to be built, would bring a great industrial and business development. I met Luther Draffen, owner and proprietor of one of Calvert City's Main Street stores in the early days—in the 1930's. The dam at Gilbertsville—later called Kentucky Dam—was on paper, and the fight to get approval and appropriations from Congress was on the way. Luther Draffen knew, in his own way, the changes a great valley development would bring. He talked; he worked; he studied. Quietly he persisted in his dream, and finally the dream was filled with substance the doubters could not deny. Kentucky Dam was built. Navigation came alive. Electricity flowed through the Valley in quantities undreamed of by the skeptics. A recreation industry—hundreds of small service enterprises—grew up around the broad waters of Kentucky Lake behind the dam, reaching across Kentucky and Tennessee from north to south.

But industries planning expansion—though frequently interested in the strategic location of the Calvert City area—somehow passed it by and grew up in other parts of the Valley. Nonetheless, the logic of Luther Draffen's ideas about the natural resources adjacent to the town and its strategic location near a waterway, railroads, and low-cost power and of its accessibility to the markets of the North and South was soon to be recognized by others.

The first to come was the Pennsylvania Salt Manufacturing Company, long a pioneer among the basic chemical industries of the country. In 1948 Penn Salt built a two-million-dollar hydrofluoric acid plant to be close to the large fluorspar deposits it had acquired in western Kentucky and to use electric power from TVA's Kentucky Dam. Next came the Pittsburgh Metallurgical Company, whose new electrolytic ferroalloys plant counts electric energy as one of the prime ingredients of its end product. By 1951 the Air Reduction Company, a big producer of industrial gases and welding equipment, started to build, through its National Carbide division, a ten-million-dollar calcium carbide and acetylene plant. Power to heat the electric furnaces of its basic operations is a big factor in production costs. A new chlorine plant, a heavy power user, was added by Penn Salt, followed by the B. F. Goodrich Chemical Company with a plant to produce plastics using hydrogen chloride from Penn Salt and acetylene from National Carbide. And near by, at Paducah, a new atomic-energy plant began to rise from the plain along the Ohio.

Here is an example of industrial integration to form a nucleus of basic chemical production, inviting expansion and growth. The construction of the plants employed men whose farming systems had been slipping out from under them through the soil erosion that goes with a tobacco-crop system. But worse, or perhaps better, the loss of Europe as a market for dark tobacco—the specialty of western Kentucky—made tobacco farming disappear and with it the means of a tough livelihood for many. The new plants in Calvert City, now in operation, are not large employers—machines, furnaces, and pressure equipment do the work. But, in an area long accustomed to a slow but steady loss of population and jobs, the beginning of a new industrial empire is changing a trend and making people hustle to keep up with it. More than five hundred jobs in the initial operating stages of the Calvert City plants are increasing to seven hundred. And the expansions now under way will call for more. These new industries, tied together by products and power, stand midway among the markets for basic chemical products in one of the nation's fast-growing developments—a new era of chemical production.

Calvert City is growing and is making plans for the future. A new water system, new schools, new homes, a new medical clinic, and new plants are the signs of a new Calvert City as it lives its busy present and moves into a new and promising future. Luther Draffen, the townsman of deep faith, may tell you if you look him up: "When you're starting from scratch, you need everything at once; but it still takes time." Luther remembers when Calvert City had more time than it had of anything else. He is no longer called a dreamer—his long thoughts about a TVA, like those of many another local citizen in any one of dozens of Valley communities, are paying off. A river at work means men and land at work and homes where people rest and visit and make new dreams that come true.

From Nothin' to Somethin'

From another town, Decatur, Alabama, two hundred miles up river from Calvert City on the Tennessee, another local citizen and community leader could fill these pages with the dramatic story of Decatur —now emerging as one of the new industrial centers of the South. I heard him speak to the assembled experts from many lands who met in September, 1949, at the United Nations Scientific Conference on the Conservation and Utilization of Resources. The place was Lake Success, New York, in an international conference room resplendent with the flags of many nations.

Barrett Shelton, editor of the *Decatur Daily*, joined with me on that occasion to report the progress of the Tennessee Valley in these words:

Decatur . . . is a town that has come from "nothin' to somethin' " in fifteen years of a working partnership between the Tennessee Valley Authority and the people of my town.

For TVA is not a magic wand. TVA would be helpless to activate community progress without the brains and the energies of a free people. [We knew that] the old order, the old way of doing things had to change.

We had to quit thinking of reaching into other sections of the United States and subsidizing industry to come into our section. . . . We had to begin in a small way to build toward a diversified agriculture and a diversified industry.

We could never again . . . allow ourselves to be dependent upon a one-industry [railroad shops] and a one-crop [cotton] system.[5]

Then, after reciting what Decatur did and how it was done, Editor Shelton added this note: "Land building did it. Flood control did it. Navigation did it. Malaria control did it. TVA, with the other state and federal . . . agencies, their teachings activated by an intelligent and determined people, did it." And when he is asked, "Wouldn't this all have happened without a TVA?" his answer is, "It didn't."

Better Living from Better Farming

What has happened to the farms as the new industries have become a part of the Valley's economic life?

Rural areas have provided most of the labor for the new industry of the region. At the same time farming as a means of livelihood has been profoundly changed in production and income and especially in the conditions of farm living. The decline in the number of people living on the land is giving others more elbow room. New production methods, particularly for forage and livestock production, are being adopted. The land receives better care and better use. The rural community is coming into its own.

A bulletin of the agricultural extension service of one of the seven land-grant colleges of the region tells a deadpan but exciting story of the changes in farm communities in Tennessee. What started years ago in piecemeal efforts to improve this or that part of rural living—a crop system here, a home canning project there has grown into a movement for the self-advancement of whole communities. Now the civic clubs of the major cities sponsor a rural community improvement contest. More than six hundred and fifty communities—marked by no boundaries of corporate limits but by a sense of neighborhood and common cause—take part each year. Shady Valley, Doe Valley, Cash Point, Old Zion—these were some of the winners in a recent evalua-

5. Barrett Shelton, "The Decatur Story," *Proceedings of the United Nations Scientific Conference on the Conservation and Utilization of Resources, 1949* (Lake Success, N.Y., 1950), I, 376–79.

tion according to standards of measurement set by the contestants themselves.

You might see this sign along the road in Tennessee:

WELCOME
CASH POINT COMMUNITY
Test Demonstration Area

Cooperating Agencies
Tennessee Extension Service—
U.S. Department of Agriculture—
University of Tennessee
College of Agriculture—
TVA—Local Farmers

OBJECTIVES
Erosion Control—Terracing—
Lime—Phosphate—Cover Crops

FARM—HOME—COMMUNITY IMPROVEMENT

You would look in vain for the cluster of homes and buildings to identify the place to which the name applies. But the community is there—farms beyond the ridges or up the valley to the left—spread where people live and farm the land. A school, a church—maybe two or three—but not in the physical groupings with homes near by which place names frequently signify. Stop and inquire and state your purpose—to find out what Cash Point is up to—and you would soon discover the community and the sense of purpose which binds its people together.

Projects for self-improvement would be pointed out or described. You would learn about the health programs (including clinics and instruction in first aid), co-operative telephone service projects, and, of course, the co-operative association for the distribution of electricity purchased wholesale from TVA. In some communities fire-fighting groups have been formed to save homes, barns, and forests. Community buildings to serve as social centers or libraries or both, supplementing the school or church, have been built by volunteer labor.

Many of the community improvement programs grew out of the fertilizer, test-demonstration farm program sponsored by the land-grant colleges with the co-operation of TVA. Many of the organizations which formed around the test-demonstration farmers evolved into community-wide associations or clubs embracing a community objective.

The Federal Reserve Bank of Atlanta in September, 1949, devoted most of its *Monthly Review* to an account of the visit of its observer to some of the community-development programs in one Valley state—Tennessee. An excerpt makes this central point:

> A farmer standing in the midst of a newly plowed field is complimented on the condition of his land and home. "How much of this would you have done if it had not been for the Community Club?" he is asked.
>
> "If it were not for the club I would not be here at all. I was fixing to buy a place somewhere else. But when I saw how everybody here was working for each other, I decided that this is the kind of a place I want to live and bring up my children. . . . I didn't want mine to be a drag-tail farm when everyone else was improving theirs."[6]

And farmers are improving their farms. The change in agriculture is a substitution on many farms of capital and improved methods for human energy. Encouraged by the results of test-demonstration programs using TVA fertilizer (see Appendix A, "Farms, Fertilizers, and Munitions"), farmers are beginning to use quantities of fertilizers unheard of a decade ago. Livestock is increasing. So is the investment in farm machinery. The census of 1950 shows a continued decline in acres planted to corn—one of the three major row crops requiring intensive human labor in the Valley. Since 1934 acreage in row crops has dropped 16 per cent while production yields have gone up. Acres blessed with hay and pasture have increased 12 per cent. Dairying, the process that makes a farm a manufacturing center—grass to milk with less human labor—has increased 50 per cent in the last fifteen years. Since 1939 there has been a fivefold increase in the number of tractors

6. Earle L. Rauber, "Farm Community Improvement," *Monthly Review, Federal Reserve Bank of Atlanta*, XXXIV (September 30, 1949), 84.

in the Valley. The formula—"forty acres and a mule"—which once described southern farming is now out of date.

In 1933 only one farm in twenty-eight had electricity! Today, nine out of ten farms have the glorious benefits of mobile, low-cost, convenient electric energy.

These advances are a good portent of more that *can* happen if the mounting initiative of the people of the Valley is permitted to move ahead. More industry is needed. A continued advance in farm improvement is essential. The closer tie between agriculture and industry is only a betrothal vow. Abundant low-cost electricity and the machine make part-time farming and factory employment more feasible. This arrangement, which joins human energies more effectively to the land and to the factory, is in its trial period. The best is yet to come. Technical guidance for part-time farmers based upon careful research in the ways and means involved in these new economic patterns will help. A strong TVA will continue to be a friendly and persistent catalytic agent for the coming union of land and machines—to "touch and give life to all forms of human concerns," as Franklin D. Roosevelt said in his 1933 message to Congress inviting the Authority to be born.

The Valley Plans Its Future

Behind these results are many examples of the multitude of efforts in which citizens by the thousands and scores of separate agencies and institutions have come together to work toward common ends in the Tennessee Valley. Farmers, businessmen, bankers, and labor leaders are working together as directors on many of the local power boards to oversee the distribution of electricity to houses no longer dark at set of sun. Farmers in many small watersheds within the Valley have joined with one another and with their counterparts in twenty-nine states to experiment with and test new forms of fertilizer and to report their results to the nation. County library boards have co-operated across county lines to administer book service in several counties as a single unit and, joining with others, have prevailed on state legislatures to extend the service to more and more areas of the state. Six state universities have combined their efforts to study the administration of natural resources in each of the states as background for recommendations to their respective governors on the organization of state functions in that field. In all these examples—and there are many more—one important theme is repeated over and over: the administrative agencies of a region are joining hands to expand public knowledge of the region's resources and to encourage people to act upon what is known. The common goal is better living for more people.

TVA does not profess to know what the *optimum population* of the Tennessee Valley should be; the facts are not all in for such a judgment. But both the people of the Valley and the TVA are reasonably confident that the economic potentialities of the region are capable of supporting a larger population at a higher level of income. As the people of the Valley push ahead to close the gap between their income and the national average, every community and every agency that has a part in this task can encourage more and more citizens to share in the planning and development of new opportunities. For, unless the planning and development of an expanding economy are shared by more and more citizens in all walks of life, the experts, in their zeal for change and a fascinating statistical result, will begin to decide what choices the seeker of employment should be permitted to make.

People in the Tennessee Valley had so few choices twenty years ago that the basic task of harnessing the river, of building power lines and carrying electricity to the farms, and of rebuilding the soil provided challenging opportunities that satisfied many unfilled elementary wants. In the last twenty years the region has moved to a new base. It has acquired and created some new dynamics. The twenty-fold increase in the amount of electric energy flowing through the life and economy of the region is, by itself, a striking index of the change that has taken place. As the Valley faces the future, the possibilities and opportunities for further development need to be analyzed more precisely. And in this task the work of twenty years in establishing and using methods that invite more local and state initiative may prove to be TVA's greatest contribution to the people of the Valley and to the world. For in the espousal and practice of this democratic process lies assurance that the voices of more and more individuals will speak up to take a share of the new opportunities and new responsibilities in a fast-growing region. The people of the Valley will thus, more and more, determine the purpose and pace of their future development. Some of the methods TVA has fostered to make this more than a promise are described in the next chapter.

IV. TVA and the States

Introduction

The Tennessee Valley Authority lives and works in a region where the emphasis upon state rights is not of recent origin. Critics outside the region sometimes refer to the Authority as a "superstate," an example of authoritarian power imposed upon helpless states. But people in the region generally laugh off such nonsense; they see in TVA a symbol for a greater Tennessee Valley. And some have even hailed it as the nation's belated compensation for the humiliations imposed upon the South during the grim years of the Reconstruction.

TVA emerged from a long history of differing views as to where to rest the responsibilities for resource conservation and development among the federal, state, and local governments. The Act of 1933 is replete with language and ideas recognizing the role of the states in the task of rebuilding the Tennessee Valley. In the light of American history this new method of intergovernmental co-operation may be viewed as an illuminating example of creative federalism.

The idea that conservation of natural resources is a matter of public concern goes back to the beginning of our national history. An early concept held that responsibility for conservation could be divided neatly between the federal and state governments, each with a clearly defined part of the task, each keeping out of the way of the other. But natural resources do not arrange themselves to fit such legalistic precision. The more realistic concept of a federal-state partnership in conservation activities and resource development has become established only in the last few decades. This idea was given current expression by President Eisenhower in his State of the Union message in

January, 1954: "Part of our Nation's precious heritage is its natural resources. It is the common responsibility of Federal, State, and local governments to improve and develop them, always working in the closest harmony and partnership."[1]

TVA and the states have exemplified this method and sought this goal for twenty years. Jointly they have invented practical arrangements suited to the particular problems which bring them together. The growth and evolution of the methods, the wealth of innovation devoid of doctrinal mental blocks, and the results of co-operative relationships between TVA and the states in and around the Tennessee Valley are the subject of this chapter.

The conservation movement has not always rested on principles of intergovernmental co-operation. Conservation as spearheaded by Theodore Roosevelt at the beginning of the present century was notable for its recognition of the interdependence of our natural resources, that is to say, among water and land and forests. This idea was reflected in comprehensive fashion for the first time, on a large scale at least, in the Tennessee Valley program. But the pioneers of the conservation movement and their successors also asserted a paramount *national* interest in our natural resources. The Federal Water Power Act passed by Congress in 1920, to take a single example, provided for federal retention and control over the development of power sites in the public domain, an idea implied in a veto message by Theodore Roosevelt as early as 1903.

A contrasting insistence on paramount rights of the states was forcibly laid down by the governor of New York, Alfred E. Smith, in 1924: "While it is true that the Federal Water Power Act gave the state the preference, it, nevertheless, attempted to establish as a fundamental principle the belief that the ultimate ownership of [water power sites] rested with the Federal Government. . . . This principle we deny and, I believe, rightly so."[2]

1. *The State of the Union* (House Doc. 251 [83d Cong., 2d sess. (Washington, D.C., 1954)]), p. 9.

2. "The Stake of the Public," *Survey*, LI (March 1, 1924), 576.

The position taken by Governor Smith was occasioned by debate over development of the St. Lawrence Waterway and led in 1931 to the creation of the New York Power Authority sponsored by another governor of New York, Franklin D. Roosevelt. This action called for *state* control over the development of water resources in the Niagara and St. Lawrence rivers within New York State. This view is not only very much alive in New York State today; it is also backed by financial resources[3] sufficient to apply it with federal capital assistance.

The emergency atmosphere of 1933 seems now, in retrospect, a strange time for a compromise on the federal-state issue regarding natural resources. Highly centralized planning to combat the depression was the keynote of the day. Under the circumstances then prevailing, it is noteworthy, indeed, that the TVA Act in many of its specific provisions called for co-operation among the federal, state, and local governments in the development of natural resources. For the first time an administrative agency was created with instructions to promote actively a federal-state relationship for regional development along lines more recently spoken of as a partnership.

It is also noteworthy that this new federal-state relationship in resource development was to be achieved by regional administrative decentralization. It involved a new kind of decentralization. Regional offices of federal departments usually mark federal responsibility grown too large to be administratively contained in Washington. Regional offices recommend, but headquarters in Washington decide. In the case of TVA, however, the board of directors was placed by law in the region. The decisions of the board were to be made where the work was to be done. This was genuine decentralization. It likewise promoted close co-operation with the states.

Three characteristics of the Tennessee Valley Authority have had considerable bearing upon its relationships to the federal government and the states. It is a multiple-purpose agency, cutting across tradi-

3. The problem and possibility in this case might be different were the flow of the Niagara and St. Lawrence dependent upon huge reservoirs to be built where nature has already provided them in the Great Lakes.

tional functional lines of the departments and agencies of the federal government in Washington. Its special responsibilities flow to one region of the nation, effectively discharged only as the regional agency can act without being subjected to veto power vested in federal departments having nation-wide programs. Finally, it is heavily flavored with a large business-type operation, which requires for its success a high degree of managerial flexibility. These three characteristics have been preserved by permitting the Authority to work as an independent agency, under a corporate form, outside the federal departmental structure, deriving its administrative status from a broadly conceived statutory charter. These attributes have given TVA the opportunity to plow new ground in the field of federal-state relationships.

Direct assistance to state agencies by TVA, including financial assistance, has often been found necessary to get a particular activity started, to demonstrate its value, and to lend support to the state or local agency in charge of its administration. As an activity proves its value to the people, and as the state or local agency grows in strength, the scale of direct assistance can generally be reduced.

This process may be illustrated by referring to one small but important activity. When the Authority builds dams, usually in an area remote from large cities, it pays funds to the state or counties to make library and book service available in construction areas. (I assume it is not necessary to explain why it is considered important that employees building a dam should be able to borrow books if they want to—and none is burned intentionally.) As a result of these arrangements a number of regional libraries were organized and operated by the states or counties to serve the construction centers. For the same cost TVA would have incurred by providing the service directly to its employees, the counties reached their own people as well. As dams were finished and workers disbanded, the Authority's financial contribution ended. But library service went right on and expanded, with financial responsibility assumed by the state and local governments. Here is a summary by dollars: In 1943 in the state of Tennessee, $18,000 was spent on regional library services, of which local sources provided $4,000 and TVA $14,000. The state contributed no funds. Ten years later $295,000 went into this same service; $125,000 came from local funds, and the state provided $170,000. The Authority contributed no funds at all.[4]

In a more general way the results of this method of initial stimulation and subsequent withdrawal of financial support are suggested by the following facts: Starting in 1934, TVA's expenditures for resource development activities carried on in co-operation with the seven states in the area gradually increased to reach an all-time high of $7.5 million in 1947. Since that time its expenditures for these activities have declined; last year they were approximately $3 million. State expenditures for resource development in the seven states were only about $10 million a year in the early period of TVA's operations. By 1947, the high point of TVA's expenditures, annual state expenditures had reached $30 million—almost four dollars by the states for every one dollar from TVA. For 1953 state resource expenditures may be estimated at about $70 million—a ratio of more than twenty to one. These figures reflect growing state responsibility and initiative in the entire field of resource development, built in many instances upon initial financial and technical assistance from the Authority.

One of the first annual reports prepared by TVA recognized that the task of rebuilding the river had been intrusted to it—but that the Valley's future development rested on the co-operative work of many agencies and individuals. To this end, a loose but effective coalition constituting the machinery of regional development has evolved. These relations could be illustrated by reference to many subjects— freight-rate equalization, in which careful joint research with the states gave the southern governors a factual basis for seeking national action; malaria control, where a complex program initiated and led by TVA with state and county agencies participating has almost eliminated malaria throughout the region; and so on through a long list. The partnership with the land-grant colleges, the state agricultural

4. Martha Parks, "A Decade of Progress: Tennessee's Regional Library Service," *Tennessee Librarian*, VI (October, 1953), 9.

extension services, and experiment stations is also an important chapter in any such recital. But there are other important examples; I have selected three for brief discussion: forestry, regional research, and electric-power distribution.

Forestry

The 14,000,000 acres of forest land in the Tennessee Valley provide the raw material for a $350 million annual business and afford protective cover for more than half of the watershed. This was once the leading hardwood lumber area of the world. After more than a century of agricultural and industrial development, 54 per cent of the land area of the Valley is still forested, and it is estimated that an additional million acres not now in timber production might be reforested to achieve the best land use. Improved management together with reforestation can restore the region to its former importance in the hardwood industry.

Present-day forests of the Valley support thousands of industries—over five thousand sawmills and fifteen hundred other plants using wood as a raw material. The number of sawmills and other wood-using plants has more than doubled since 1935. But, with all its apparent economic productiveness, the forest resource of the Valley is yielding far below its capability. Total wood capital in standing trees could be increased three times. Annual wood growth also could be trebled. If this much wood were available to industry, income from this resource could be increased from $350 million to $1 billion annually.

The Tennessee Valley, like many other forest areas, illustrated the tragic cycle of destructive forest, soil, and water losses which follow "cut-and-run" timber practice. In the early history of TVA, suggestions were made to its board to buy large acreages of forest lands and to seek legislation to introduce some measure of regulation over forest landowners. The board rejected both ideas. It was clear that no one agency or the states alone could stop and reverse this cycle. A program for the Tennessee Valley drainage area as a whole was required.

The forestry agencies of the states, the United States Forest Service, and many landowners knew what ought to be done, but they needed help. The Authority provided leadership and joined with them in a four-point program based on these major premises:

1. Increased protection against fire was the first and most obvious need.

2. Better forest management and cutting practices, on farm woodlands as well as on large industrial timber tracts, would improve yields and assure the growth of the future crop.

3. Thousands of acres of eroding, idle lands needed reforestation.

4. Development of wood-using industries and extension of new processes to utilize lower-grade timber would help to make good forest management pay off and provide additional employment.

Within the seven Valley states many public agencies are now working toward these objectives. Those most intimately concerned are the state departments of conservation. Each of these seven state agencies has a definite legislative mandate in the field of forest development. All have joined wholeheartedly in the Valley program. Through the mediation of the Authority, state agricultural extension services also help to promote better forestry practices on farm woodlands. County agents spent only 74 man-days on farm forestry work in 1933 compared to more than 1,000 man-days in 1953. Federal agricultural agencies have lent valuable assistance to the states and counties, especially in reforestation. Central to all, regional in its interest, and using stimulative financial assistance, demonstrations, research projects, and a staff skilled in the art of practical interpretation and persuasion has been TVA's Division of Forestry Relations.

What are the results of this approach thus far?

Forest-fire control has been organized and is being financed through federal, state, and local co-operation. Ninety-seven of the Valley's 125 counties are co-operating financially in this program as compared with 8 counties in 1934. The forest area under organized protection now is 12,500,000 acres, or about 89 per cent of the total forest area.

More than four hundred demonstrations of scientific forest-management practices on a total of some 130,000 acres have been established with landowners. These demonstrations range from small farm woodlands to large industrial forest holdings. More than 200,000 acres have been reforested with 156,000,000 trees provided by TVA since 1933. Some fifteen thousand farmers have demonstrated that serious erosion can be effectively controlled by reforestation. The Valley-wide inventory of the forest resource and the census of wood-using industries, compiled and kept current by the Authority, have helped hundreds of timber operators and industries, large and small, to find the specific kinds of timber stands they needed; new industries have been established; and many communities have been assisted in making plans for industrial development based upon the facts about their timber resources available for the first time in these detailed inventories.

Numerous timber trade associations are joined in this coalition, because forests provide raw material for the industries they represent. Sawmill operators go to school in demonstration meetings to learn how to improve efficiency, reduce wood waste, earn more money, and leave a better forest behind them. Now that forestry is becoming good business, private professional foresters have entered the field, retained by landowners for expert assistance and advice. Many lay groups, banded together by a deep interest in forests or wildlife, are molding public opinion in favor of forest conservation and exerting constructive support toward improvement in the management of natural resources.

These results are but a beginning. The major importance of what has been accomplished is found in the methods by which forest development can be promoted on a voluntary basis. These results have been achieved without the exercise of any power of coercion. There has been no invasion of the property rights of landowners; TVA has not encroached upon the responsibility or functions of the state and local governments. In fact, the state forest agencies are becoming stronger than ever before.

The seven state divisions of forestry, for example—those branches of the state conservation departments charged with forest protection and development—in fiscal year 1935 operated on funds totaling about

$500,000. For fiscal year 1952 their expenditures amounted to almost $8 million. Technical personnel increased from 36 to 300. In 1935 these agencies were occupied primarily with forest-fire suppression; 70 per cent of their total funds was spent on fighting fires or getting ready to fight them. Fire suppression is still a big job, but the annual burn is gradually being reduced. And today 80 per cent of the total funds available to the forestry agencies of the seven states goes for positive measures of forest development rather than fire suppression.

The Valley's forests are a better resource now than in 1933, but the job is far from done. Continued progress will depend upon expanding public support for more money and better personnel for the state forestry agencies, with TVA continuing in the background to encourage and assist in the attainment of a regional goal.

Regional Research

The wise development of natural resources cannot be accomplished without intelligent research. A region needs to build strong agencies for research—agencies whose work will inform the people, broaden the area of their choice, and let regional development proceed on the basis of knowledge and a richer experience. Where research budgets are limited as they are in the Tennessee Valley states, especially in the social sciences, co-operation among research groups can compound the values of information and knowledge and increase the utility of the research dollar.

A few examples in the field of social studies will illustrate a pattern of co-operative research in the Tennessee Valley which extends into a number of fields and includes hundreds of projects. Studies of municipal government and administration were made to provide practical background information for the power-distribution systems of the cities using TVA electricity. The university bureaus of public administration, organized in several instances for the purpose of making these studies, were financed by TVA. Their programs were continued and expanded by the states after completion of the initial co-operative projects. The bureaus of business research in the region have likewise co-operated in the study of regional problems, such as the analysis of county income, in which a new methodology was devised and tried successfully.

In 1944 six state universities joined with TVA in an interstate project which at the time was unique to the region and perhaps anywhere: a study of the administrative organizations and programs of the states relating to natural resources. The research facilities at the several universities were supplemented by a General Education Board grant. Regional meetings of research personnel were held to develop a joint approach suitable for all the participating states. Work conferences compared findings and exchanged ideas. The pattern of co-operation in research thus established carried over into a whole series of joint undertakings. The institutions have formed a continuing organization now known as the Southern Public Administration Research Council. It no longer depends for support upon TVA's financing, although it continues to have the co-operation and participation of the Authority's research personnel.

Another example of co-operative research illustrates the multiple by-products of the regional approach. Each of the Valley states maintains a Negro land-grant college. Until recently these colleges have been concerned mostly with vocational fields of study; research in the social sciences was not an important part of their work, and yet the people they served were passing through a period of great economic and occupational change. Members of the college professional staffs had little contact with each other, with the white land-grant colleges, or with regional development programs. Their isolated existence challenged the theory of a regional partnership for research and education. Here was a relatively unused regional resource which might be strategically equipped to take leadership in studying the needs of an important part of the region's population, largely centered in rural areas but moving rapidly into the cities. And the Authority certainly needed to know the dimensions and nature of this change.

Beginning in 1948 with Tuskegee Institute, TVA has provided modest support for social science research in this group of colleges.

The method, developed through the Conference of Presidents, has encouraged joint projects among the member colleges, under the supervision of a research director, and brought research personnel together in regional meetings from time to time. Through this program the Negro colleges have gained greater recognition by the other colleges. There has also been a tenfold increase in the annual social science research budgets of the seven colleges taking part in the program.

The Tennessee Valley region needs personnel and facilities for more research. Budgets are low, and staffs are generally too small for even the most obvious needs. However, co-operation and the opportunity for joint study have led many institutions to establish better research facilities and to make them useful to their respective states and to the region.[5]

Federal-Local Partnership for Electric Service

A recital of how TVA and the states work together cannot omit what is perhaps the outstanding example of a true partnership—the generation and distribution of electricity serving an area about the size of England and Scotland. This great public power arrangement is sometimes referred to as an example of creeping encroachment by the federal government upon the sovereignty of the states and an attempt to reduce the cities to the status of dejected and helpless captives. Nothing ever said about the Authority could be further from the truth.

In the next two chapters I shall dwell upon the broad human and national significance of elecricity in some detail. But I ask you now to reflect upon this example of relationships among governments through

5. The role of TVA in this field has been described by others in these words: "If the Tennessee Valley Authority has been cooperative . . . with the Alabama Bureau [of Public Administration], it likewise has the satisfaction of knowing that its cooperation has secured tangible results in the form of research reports with a cash-in-hand value many times the TVA contribution. TVA can also take credit for helping to set in motion forces throughout the area . . . for the scientific study of political and administrative life in the region the implications of which run far beyond the necessarily transient significance of the contemporary research programs of the newly established or revitalized bureaus of public administration" (Rowland Egger and Weldon Cooper, *Research, Education, and Regionalism* [University, Ala.: University of Alabama, Bureau of Public Administration, 1949], pp. 212–13).

the device of a network of contracts, a hundred and fifty in number, which join together, voluntarily, a great body of towns, cities, and rural communities in a complex public service enterprise.

TVA produces large quantities of electric power. The Act provides that this power be used to serve the interests of the people of the Tennessee Valley and the national defense. The board early announced its intention, subject to limited and temporary exceptions, not to engage in the retail distribution of electricity. Its power function, in the main, would be limited to the generation and transmission of electrical energy, with delivery of power at wholesale to the lines of distribution agencies that would in turn serve the ultimate consumers.

In the sale of power the law prescribed that preference be given "to States, counties, municipalities, and cooperative organizations of citizens or farmers, not organized or doing business for profit, but primarily for the purpose of supplying electricity to its own citizens or members." The Act also provides that power be sold "at the lowest possible rates . . . to encourage increased domestic and rural use of electricity."[6]

The states in the area enacted special legislation authorizing their cities to establish municipal systems and to enter into power contracts with the Authority. Most of the cities now distributing its power held referendums to decide what course to follow. The legal arrangements developed in Mississippi and Alabama for the rural distribution of electricity through consumer co-operatives set the pattern for state enabling acts which later accommodated rural electric co-operatives in most of rural America. Today TVA electricity is being distributed to consumers over practically all the state of Tennessee and in parts of six neighboring states by 97 separate municipal power systems, 51 rural electric co-operatives, and 2 small, local systems in private ownership.

This bare outline of events gives a deceptively simple picture of the development of a far-flung public power system—the largest single integrated system in the United States. It serves more than 1,300,000

6. Act of May 18, 1933, Secs. 10–11 (48 Stat. 64–65).

retail consumers, representing a population of 5,000,000 people spread over an area of some 80,000 square miles. In the legal sense TVA's relations with local power distributors are governed by formal contracts by which it becomes the exclusive source of electric-energy supply for resale by distributors at rates agreed upon by both parties. But many, many questions were posed and worked out in the evolution of this public enterprise. The negotiation of each contract, the joint purchase and redivision of former private power-company properties among the Authority and the local power systems, the delineation of retail service areas, the organization of municipal power boards and rural electric co-operatives—these and hundreds of other problems have been the subject of discussion and negotiation. Legislative committees and public utility commissions, state municipal leagues, city councils, county courts, the President of the United States, Congress, and citizen groups in towns and rural areas have all had a hand in shaping the result.

Whenever conflicts arise—as they have and will—compromise must be considered and solution achieved within the broad framework of the public interest in the largest sense of the term. If agreement cannot be reached, the courts are open to either party, a recourse followed only twice in twenty years. And on one important occasion a long study and negotiation among the states, the counties, and TVA produced a plan for revision of the payments the Authority makes to states and counties in lieu of taxes to replace those formerly obtained from reservoir lands and utility properties, and the Act was accordingly amended. The plan for payments in lieu of taxes and the process by which it was developed stand high in the list of examples of how federal, state, and local governments can weigh and resolve equitably local, regional, and national interests.

Here is an illustration, by the way, of the peculiar responsibility of a *regional* agency as it faces in two directions—toward the region and toward the nation. When TVA and the cities and rural electric co-operatives joined to acquire the utility properties of the private companies operating in the region (an acquisition approved by Congress and the President), valuable private property was removed from the tax base of the counties in which several small dams and other electric facilities were located. In a few sparsely populated counties in the mountains the private utility property was the major tax source for county schools. It was recognized that the formula in the original TVA Act for payments in lieu of taxes to states and counties should be changed. But how much?

A careful study was made. With the facts in hand, there were meetings with governors, tax and finance commissioners, and county magistrates to appraise the analysis and to negotiate a proposal to be submitted to the President and Congress as an amendment to Section 13 of the Act.

In these negotiations the counties pressed for the highest possible payments that could be extracted from the power revenues of TVA. The states were interested in the financial needs of the counties, to be sure, but they also had their own budgetary problems—they wanted their share. At the same time both parties were aware of the mounting benefits accruing to the area through the power system. New dams, new employment, new lakes with great recreation possibilities, and new industry were increasing the property value and the tax base within the states and counties. And TVA's revenues are an asset to the federal government, providing a return on the investment made by the nation's taxpayers. The Authority, therefore, had to face two ways—to assure an equitable adjustment between the claims of states and counties and the federal taxpayers' rightful expectation of a return on their investment in the power system.

In the hearings and debates in Congress interesting inconsistencies developed. Some spokesmen from outside the Tennessee Valley urged that TVA be required to pay more to the states and counties in spite of the fact such payments would reduce the amount it would otherwise pay from its power revenues into the general fund of the United States Treasury. Governors and county magistrates were somewhat puzzled by this unexpected concern for their welfare until they realized that the private utilities were trying to load the Authority's payment burden in order to break the wholesale and resale rates for electricity. Others inside and outside the area argued that the new plan would pay too much to the states and counties and thereby reduce cash payments to the federal treasury.

But the amendment as passed incorporated the plan as developed by negotiation and study in the region. The facts and the careful process of negotiation survived an extremely close scrutiny by Congress. The proposal was judged to be fair to electric consumers, states and counties of the region, as well as to the nation's taxpayers.

The understanding and informed relationship between TVA and municipal and co-operative power distributors may be illustrated again by the successful negotiation last year of an upward adjustment of wholesale rates and resale rates for power to industrial customers. Rates for residential and small consumers were not revised. The need for increasing industrial rates had been brought about by the addition of new steam plants to the system, a higher-cost source of power than the dams. These steam plants, available for continuous operation, fit the supply requirements of high-load factor industries, operating around the clock the year round.

Let me cite the following fact as a measure of the true partnership of these arrangements in the Tennessee Valley. In this public power partnership, local distribution agencies through issuance of revenue bonds and use of surplus earnings have invested in their systems about $400 million. This amount is roughly equivalent to that part of TVA's federal investment in generating and transmission properties which serve municipal and co-operative loads, subtracting that portion of the federal investment required to provide power for national defense.

Some Current Problems

Several special problems have been cited in which the achievement of interagency co-operation has been useful or essential and is now well established. New fields of co-operation continue to emerge as problems change and public interest becomes informed. I would like to select two illustrations for brief description: local flood control and the intensive development of tributary watersheds.

Local flood control.—Through a system of large dams and reservoirs TVA is able to control floods on the Tennessee River and its important tributaries. This system prevents major floods at especially critical points in the Valley. Half of its flood-control benefits accrue outside the Valley on the lower Ohio and lower Mississippi as far south as the mouth of the Red River. There remain, however, many local flood problems of lesser magnitude within the Valley. Because the dams control the major floods, many of the remaining smaller flood dangers have been brought within the range of remedies the states and local communities can apply. There are also a number of local flood problems not affected by the main river system and which do not contribute to major floods. But these little floods are serious locally when they happen.

Careful study of stream flow over the years has provided a basis for classifying flood areas in the Tennessee Valley to distinguish between floods of local significance only and those which affect the region by contributing to floods on the Tennessee. The Authority is directly concerned with both types, but its responsibility in each case is different. As experience accumulates in the management of the flood-control system, a local flood-control program in the Tennessee Valley moves into a position of higher priority. The solution lies in a co-operative approach between TVA and the states and the local communities.

Operation of the water-control system requires systematic collection of information on rainfall and stream flow and on the nature, pattern, and magnitude of past floods. Over the years there have been established effective arrangements with state and local planning agencies by which this information is shared for local application. The states are now being encouraged to develop a new concept of assistance which will suggest ways and means by which local agencies or groups may accept responsibility for a local program with technical help from the state and TVA.

What is now described is a program only partly formed and partly planned. But the methods and the objectives are clear. In the Tennessee Valley local flood control is being considered as an essential part of local planning and development, with the Authority and state agencies supplying data and technical assistance as needed. Such studies may lead to local control of land use by means of zoning and subdivision regulations in areas subject to flood, the protection of the river channel against encroachment, and the application of flood-control data to such administrative decisions as road location and extension of utilities. Protective local flood-control structures, such as levees, are considered within the context of a more comprehensive pattern of actions by which the community adjusts itself to flood conditions and rearranges the disposal of flood waters.

The control of localized floods will not be achieved except as it becomes a part of the whole subject of regional and community development. During the last two decades technical and political thinking has been so dominated by the cost-benefit question that many have been encouraged to believe local flood prevention to be synonymous with dams and levees. Another school of thought asserts, erroneously, that better land use, more cover, terraces, forests, etc., near the headwaters of a stream will make big dams unnecessary. Both schools of thought— dams alone versus land-use measures alone—are usually wrong. There is no substitute for dams and levees to control great floods. The scale of the big floods is greater than sod and forest can control. But these devices for handling large-scale movements are the prelude to a vast, far-reaching complex catalogue of tailor-made arrangements in individual communities—arrangements of academic consequence unless the major flood-control system cuts the big floods down to manageable size for states, towns, and cities.

Repeatedly we see encroachment by homes, stores, and factories into areas known to be subject to damaging floods. Partial protection by federally constructed dams and levees alone often encourages further development along the flood plain and in turn creates renewed damands for further protection. The local flood reports commonly prepared by the Army Engineers usually have as their central theme a recommendation for the construction of protective works or the verdict that the benefits in prospect are not worth the cost. Community action is then too frequently limited to promotional efforts in support or in rebuttal of the recommendations of the technical report. Delegations of local citizens move on Washington. There may be another survey, another report, another conclusion laying the basis for federal money if the community will furnish the right of way for levees and promises to share the cost of maintenance. The scene then shifts back home, where memory of the flood has receded, financial and land commitments fail to materialize, and the hoped-for plan goes into the files—authorized but dormant until the next flood hits. In the meantime the local government does nothing about the danger. Another flood comes, bringing damage and disaster in its wake. Relief then becomes an immediate cost—frequently equivalent to the costs of preventing a flood.

The key to this problem is that local agencies should be made responsible for the flood-protection remedy it is within their power to apply. Their function should not be limited to that of promoting a levee, a dike, or a dam. Each situation is different and requires careful and comprehensive analysis to find the proper preventive measures. Local flood problems require an understanding of the nature and extent of the flood conditions and of the action which communities can take without major federal assistance if the problem is to be solved. Local communities need technical assistance, and the states are the logical place for them to obtain it. But states need help, too, and TVA is prepared to help the states to establish and equip their own agencies to provide such service to their towns and cities. This is the new pattern of responsibilities emerging in the Tennessee Valley. But, as long as the road from the local community to Washington is open, by-passing the state, progress will be slow.

Tributary watersheds.—Intensive as a regional program may be, its effects vary greatly among areas within the region. A number of watersheds whose streams flow into the Tennessee system have lagged behind the region's economic and physical advance. TVA, therefore, has long visualized these little river valleys as a small proto-type of the Tennessee Valley as it was a decade or two ago. It has long looked forward to the time when the major Valley-wide tasks would be well in hand so that it might concentrate on these special areas. Perhaps what has worked for the Valley as a whole can be ap-plied more intensively within these underdeveloped tributary water-sheds.

The first co-operative program for the development of a small watershed in the Tennessee Valley was started on Chestuee Creek, Tennessee, in 1951. Chestuee is a tributary of the Hiwassee—a tribu-tary of the Tennessee. It is an area of 135 square miles and involves three counties. This area was selected because during the war one of the county courts in the area asked TVA to dredge the Chestuee Creek so it would carry and discharge flood flows more quickly. It was explained to the county that the problem reached back to the head-waters and onto the farmers' fields and woodlands. It would be no use to dig a faster flow channel until measures of water control on the land had shown their effect.

After long discussions and studies covering far more than water, land, and engineering, a program was begun. This program is not limited to physical remedial and improvement measures; rather, it is concerned with the general economic strength and welfare of the whole watershed. In Chestuee much of the initial leadership and a large share of the financial support have been provided by TVA. Stream gauges have been placed to measure water flow, the number of test-demonstration farms has been increased, and forestry improve-ment work and the demonstration of farm uses of electricity have been intensified in this watershed. But a heavy battery of state and local agencies is also at work in this special pilot-plant program: the state university, the state health department, the state department of educa-tion, the state division of forestry, the state highway department, local schools, teachers' and community organizations, and other local groups. As the program continues, it is expected that a larger share of the responsibility will be assumed by state and local agencies. Indeed, the most important measure of the success of the Chestuee program lies in the rate of speed by which the activities find more and more financial support from the counties and the state.

With Chestuee as a proving ground, TVA awaits adaptation of this program in similar tributary watersheds in other parts of the Valley. It has urged the state to take full responsibility for leadership in spreading the idea, with the Authority relegated to a less conspicuous role. In western Tennessee the people of the Beech River watershed, under the leadership of a local committee, are eager to follow Chestuee's example. TVA has surveyed the area, analyzed some of the major physical and economic problems, and suggested possible solutions in a report filed and discussed with the local committee and the governor.

The governor, after studying the problem with his staff, has recently indicated that the state is prepared to go ahead. If this program goes forward in Beech River, Tennessee will be among the first of the states to embark on a comprehensive program of local watershed development going far beyond the scope of the soil-conservation, little-valley demonstrations now inviting large federal expenditures. It is hoped that a similar response will come from adjoining states with watersheds tributary to the Tennessee. TVA believes that state leadership and technical assistance in these local problems are appropriate—indeed, imperative. Here is an opportunity for the states to rearrange relationships between local communities and the nation's capital, to energize the latent leadership in those special areas whose problems are too severe and resources too small to go it alone. What they need is informed attention and technical assistance under the leadership of their own state governments. Here indeed is a fertile field for the intensive cultivation of a new type of state and local co-operation.

Conclusion

The search for effective methods and techniques of co-operation among local, state, and federal governments must never end. The experience in the Tennessee Valley gives new emphasis to an observation Woodrow Wilson made many years ago:

The question of the relation of the States to the federal government is the cardinal question of our constitutional system. . . . It cannot . . . be settled by the opinion of any one generation, because it is a question of growth, and every successive stage of our political and economic development gives it a new aspect, makes it a new question.[7]

The story of TVA and the states is constantly changing. As a part of the national scene, it is a continuing experiment in the regional decentralization of federal functions. In the light of present national trends the Valley's experience assumes new importance. This governmental partnership in the field of resource development has wide application and is ripe for emulation.

The program to conserve natural resources among the state and local governments in the Tennessee Valley has inspired and encouraged new concepts of stewardship for our natural resources. New activities of government have evolved and found understanding support among local taxpayers; old tasks have been performed more effectively.

For TVA this experience has been both difficult and rewarding, the prospects of the future both sobering and challenging. The methods I have described do not bring quick or dramatic results. There is always a temptation to take short cuts, to by-pass the states when their agencies are understaffed and their staffs underpaid. When people generally seem to be complacent about our disappearing natural resources, a few become impatient with the co-operative process and urge agencies of the federal government to do the job *for* the people, a course that fosters still more complacency on the part of citizens. The purpose of the co-operative processes I have described is to foster interest and action by individuals and communities in conserving and using wisely our natural resources.

A true partnership implies freedom to disagree. It accords the people of a region not only a choice among certain courses of action but the right to reject assistance or, if they choose, to do nothing at all. The partnership between TVA and the region does not exist in an

7. *Constitutional Government in the United States* (New York: Columbia University Press, 1908), p. 173.

absence of conflict. Successful experience begets understanding and confidence; and as the process of co-operation proceeds from function to function, from program to program, it becomes progressively less difficult. It rests upon tested methods and a proved capacity to reduce potential conflicts of interest and to bring them within reach of agreement in the regional and national interest. The process is not easy; it requires hard work, imagination, and an abiding good will among the participants.

Professor Leonard D. White of the University of Chicago wrote in 1953: "If the states can take the initiative in these hard years to preserve and to strengthen their place in the federal structure, they may have won victories that will stand long in the memory of man."[8] At the heart of this problem lies the need for devices of federal-state co-operation. If TVA, as a national regional agency, is permitted to continue to work in partnership with the states to bring new substance and new processes into the grand scheme of federal-state co-operation, it will have served well our rich heritage of federalism.

8. *The States and the Nation* (Baton Rouge: Louisiana State University Press, 1953), p. 101.

V. Too Little Electricity

Introduction and Summary

The controversy about public or private ownership of electric-power facilities has diverted the nation's attention from a more fundamental question. *Adequacy* of power for our country's needs—irrespective of ownership—is today a pressing, indeed, a vital, issue. That is what I propose to discuss in this and the following chapter. My thesis is this:

1. An ample supply of electrical energy at the lowest attainable cost is a basic force that stimulates the expansion of economic activity in a competitive enterprise society.

2. The present expansion of power-generating facilities, large though it be, is not enough; it does not assure the country an adequate power supply in the years ahead.

3. Maintenance of our national strength to avert war and the strength to wage war if we must—our very national security—require a margin of power supply that can accommodate quickly the adjustments a modern and versatile national defense plan embodies.

4. These goals have not been and will not be achieved by sole reliance upon privately owned electric utilities. Electric-power-generating systems, whether private or public, require heavy investments per unit of revenue, making duplication of facilities very costly. That is one of the reasons why it is necessary to give power systems monopoly status in their respective areas of service. Heavy capital requirements plus lack of competition encourage private utilities to restrict expansion of generating capacity and thereby discourage greater use of electricity. Restricted consumption keeps electric costs high and in turn discourages greater use. Lower rates would increase electric

use and revenues, distribute fixed charges over a larger number of kilowatt-hours sold, and thereby help to reduce costs per unit. The country seldom has the crucial margins of power capacity sufficient to encourage and accommodate a rate of growth in production commensurate with America's opportunities. A traditional attitude of waiting for demand to precede new supply and a historical habit of discounting the prospective future growth of the country—understandable attributes inherent in the monopoly structure of the electric business—have regularly interpreted too little power as quite enough and "too late" as in good time.

5. In this last half of the twentieth century, America's responsibility as a leader in the quest for world peace and better living requires a new and bolder approach to the problem of energy supply. This approach should recognize first and foremost that the electric utilities need competition to make them do their best. Moreover, an ample power supply is so vital to national welfare and security that utilities, privately as well as publicly owned, should receive governmental assistance in meeting capital requirements. Applications of the best modern technology in power-supply development would be accelerated by such a course. The result would be greater efficiency and economy in the use of natural resources for power production and higher productivity per unit of human labor.

6. Publicly owned power systems, held accountable to a higher standard of service to the consumer, have achieved an enviable record in anticipating energy requirements. In addition, they have exhibited an enterprising spirit in fostering new uses of electricity. A policy of low rates has encouraged greater use; and this in turn has reduced costs, increased revenues and earnings, and impelled a faster rate of capacity expansion. These policies have stimulated and accelerated economic development, which in turn has crowded power supply, thus demonstrating the positive role electric energy can perform if supplied to lead, not follow, the "market." By example, public power operations have stimulated private utilities, particularly in areas where consumers were aware of the rates their neighbors were pay-

ing for electricity. The demonstration of the Tennessee Valley Authority power system, low rates, and expanding use stimulated new practices and brought profits to neighboring private utilities and expanded service to consumers. It laid a stronger energy foundation upon which national defense developments could be quickly built.

7. A concern for the national security should counsel caution in neutralizing or destroying the only influence which has so far proved effective in modifying the practices of privately owned utilities—the threat of competition in ideas about alternative ways of conducting the power business.

8. A wise national policy would nourish and hold accountable both private and public ownership in a pattern of watchful competition in performance, each encouraged in its own area of service to merit public support by its record of performance. Public ownership of our power industry, without competition from examples of private ownership, might develop the same bureaucratic inertia which has cursed the private utilities. The country needs vigorous competition in performance between privately and publicly owned systems.

9. And let no one forget that electric service is a *public* service no matter who owns and operates the properties that supply and distribute power. If the private utilities satisfy the public need for low-cost electricity in abundance, they improve their chance of staying in business. How long the private power companies remain private will depend upon how well they discharge their *public* responsibilities.

These are the propositions I shall analyze and discuss in detail in this and the next and final chapter of this book.

Electric Energy Is a Basic Necessity of Community and National Life, an Absolute Requirement for National Strength and Security

An adequate supply of electrical energy is vital in a dynamic free-enterprise economy. Since 1900 our population has doubled, our use of electricity has increased sixty-six times, and our total output of industrial goods has expanded seven times. The ever increasing reliance on electrical machinery and a greater use of energy per unit of human labor have helped to reduce the average work week by 25 per cent. Over the last fifty years the use of electric power in manufacturing has risen from less than 1 kilowatt-hour to more than 60 kilowatt-hours for every 10 man-hours of labor—a seventy-fold increase!

Electrical energy has become the prime mover in our dynamic economy. It has shaped and constantly improved the material circumstances of our lives. It has given strength and substance to America's ability to accept world leadership. Because electricity can be produced in central stations and is easily transmitted to where it is needed, it is a form of energy especially suited to motivate mass production in the industrial field. Through electrolysis and the electric furnace, in combination with the chemical industry, it has enabled us to transform idle and otherwise useless resources into economic goods.

In the twenty-five-year span from 1925 to 1950 consumption of electric energy increased four and a half times, while the total national output of goods and services approximately doubled. In the Tennessee Valley, where an ample supply of energy at low cost to all classes of consumers was a statutory goal, explicitly defined in the Act, the expansion of electric-energy supply and use has been even more phenomenal. In 1933 the area now served by TVA used 1,500,000,000 kilowatt-hours. By 1950 the same area used more than 16,000,000,000 kilowatt-hours. This represented a rate of increase of 15 per cent per year, almost double the national growth (8–9 per cent annually) over the same period. In the ten years from the end of World War II through 1955 generating capacity in this power service area will have expanded by 270 per cent, or double the national growth of 135 per cent. By the end of 1955 TVA will be producing not 1,500,000,000, not 16,000,000,000, but almost 55,000,000,000 kilowatt-hours per year.

Electric energy has reduced human toil and increased the income of farm and factory workers. In addition, it has brought conveniences and higher standards of material well-being directly into our homes. The housewife in a mountain home in the Tennessee Valley a few years ago carried water in a bucket filled from a spring or hand-pumped from a well. Several times a day—and day in and day out—the elementary uses of water to quench thirst and keep house and family clean have exacted a heavy price in human toil. Today in the Tennessee Valley more and more rural homes get water from a faucet; electric energy pumps and circulates the requirements of the family and farm livestock for two or three cents a day. Electric washing machines are replacing the backbreaking scrub board and tub; refrigeration, electric water heaters, and the electric range are transforming the requirements and outlets for human energies in manifold ways.

In a southern climate milk production becomes practical if, among other things, electric energy can supply running water for dairy sanitation and for the cooling and storage of milk.

In mountain areas where summer showers are frequent during haying season an electric hay-drier in the barn permits the harvest to proceed with less dependence upon the weather and less risk for the farmer.

In rural neighborhoods electric energy transforms the schoolhouse into a day-and-night community building; some of the time and human energy that electricity saves for people during the day are spent in more civic and social gatherings. Scattered neighborhoods become coherent communities through meetings, talk, and planning.

Electricity has had no small part in these changes. If there be those who doubt the direct and diverse effect a rural electric distribution line has on the life and living of people, if there be those who would still refer to electric energy as "a technical matter" for engineers and financiers, a few conversations with those who were once beyond the reach of electricity and now possess and use it would be persuasive.

Electricity as a necessity in rural America has taken its place with the church and school as an institution which people fight for—to establish, nourish, and expand. Those who have not recognized this as a fact will learn it one way or another.

But, aside from its contribution to material well-being, an ample supply of low-cost energy is imperative to insure our national security. Modern warfare requires unprecedented levels of output from virtually all parts of the economy. These levels of output demand maximum efficiency in the use of material and energy resources. Labor, capital, and materials must be used with maximum effectiveness. In war electric power is a strategic key to larger output per unit of raw materials and human energy.

More specifically, many critical defense items are heavily dependent upon large quantities of low-cost power. The production of fissionable materials for atomic weapons, titanium, aluminum, metal alloys, and certain chemicals requires large quantities of power. Today, the aluminum industry alone, for example, requires almost a fifth as much electricity as was consumed by the entire nation only twenty years ago. By 1956 the atomic-energy program will require about one-third as much energy as the entire economy used before World War II. With the critical role of electrical energy in the nation's defense program, an ample low-cost supply is necessary to assure the security of the nation and minimize the cost of its defense.

America Needs More Power than the Power Industry Is Preparing To Supply

Power capacity in the United States is expanding at a rate faster than at any time in our history. Does that fact suggest that we now have or are about to have enough electric power to fulfil the nation's needs for continued development of our economy and for defense requirements? The tragic fact is that the country does not have enough power now; we are not likely to have enough in the future if present trends continue. Ever since World War II, as the Edison Electric Institute, an agency of the privately owned electric utilities, has recently observed, "the Electric Utility Industry has been building to take care of growth and to catch up on wartime deferred plant expansion in order to restore reserve margins."[1]

Lagging behind the demand has become a habit for the electric util-

1. *Statistical Bulletin, Year 1952* (New York: Edison Electric Institute, 1953), p. 46.

ity industry in the United States. The situation in the twenties was summed up by the president of the National Electric Light Association, the voice of the industry at that time. In 1927 he said, "We are agreed that the electric light and power companies are not selling as much electric energy as obvious opportunities warrant."[2]

In the early thirties the industry had a margin of reserve because of the severe depression. Power surpluses were viewed with deep alarm, not as a challenge to managerial leadership to increase demand. In 1933, while testifying before the House committee in opposition to the enactment of the proposal to establish the Authority, a vice-president of Commonwealth and Southern Corporation stated that he could foresee no market at the time for the power to be produced by TVA! Yet in 1940, before the fall of France, before the era of defense production, demand in the Tennessee Valley was more than double the level of consumption the private-company official envisioned; and by 1953 it exceeded the 1933 level by seventeen times.

The tendency of the utility leaders to discount the prospects of future growth should be a source of concern and sober reflection. But the complacency with which the private utilities often have viewed national defense requirements is a cause for alarm. In 1935, when David Lilienthal appeared before the Military Affairs Committee of the House of Representatives to urge more rapid development of the latent power of the Tennessee River in response to the German rearmament program, there was no industry voice to second such a farsighted proposal. In February, 1940, before the fall of France, Mr. Lilienthal, in a public speech again stated emphatically that, unless power supply was greatly increased at once, the nation would face a shortage of electric power for defense production. A few months later C. W. Kellogg, then president of Edison Electric Institute, the official voice of the electric utility industry, sought to reassure those who would listen by declaring that "although a large national defense program stimulates not only industrial but commercial and residential

2. R. F. Pack, "The President's Page," *N.E.L.A. Bulletin*, XIV (March, 1927), 134.

business as well, *experience indicates that war itself does not accelerate an increase in the overall demand for electricity.*"[3]

In May, 1941, Mr. Lilienthal, speaking for TVA, again stated, "The time for nibbling cautiously at power supply is long since past." A few days later Mr. Kellogg, who had become chief consultant on electric power to the Office of Production Management of the federal government, again addressed himself to the question of the adequacy of power supply. He said, "Allegation of power shortage is unwarranted; . . . I believe the power situation will be found to have been adequately provided for."[4]

Within a year the gravity of this country's position with respect to power supply and the reasons for it became so obvious that a writer in *Public Utilities Fortnightly*, a trade journal not unfriendly to the private utilities, stated: "We have to remember that Mr. Kellogg speaks from the ranks of the industry [*sic*], and that the wish is often father to the thought." The article continues:

What is of supreme importance in the war effort is time. Since a power bottleneck or breakdown may be of vital importance if, for example, it delays the aircraft program at some crucial stage in the war, it is highly important that insofar as possible each power area seek to be self-sufficient and possessed of reserves for unforeseeable contingencies.

Significantly, the writer adds:

Even if we see a threat to private ownership of utilities in the war expansion program, if the alternative is to seriously weaken the nation's war potential, the risk is worth while. Indeed, there is no real alternative. Warfare today depends upon industrial power, which in turn depends upon electric power, not merely on numbers of men in uniform.[5]

The history of forecasting power requirements for the nation is marked by predictions that err with remarkable consistency on the side of understating future demands. The Federal Power Commission,

3. "The Electric Utilities Are Prepared," *Edison Electric Institute Bulletin*, VIII (June, 1940), 256. (Italics mine.)

4. "The President's Address," *Edison Electric Institute Bulletin*, IX (June, 1941), 222.

5. H. M. Bratter, "Have We Power To Do the Job?" *Public Utilities Fortnightly*, XXIX (March 26, 1942), 404, 405.

when it had a sterling reputation for safeguarding the public interest, was regarded by many in the industry as too optimistic in its projections of power requirements when it made a forecast in 1947 for the following five years.[6] Actual demand exceeded the estimate by 50 per cent. This cannot be explained by the unexpected industrial demands imposed by the Korean mobilization program, although they contributed. Residential and rural loads were also grossly underestimated. Within a year after the forecasts, actual load in residential and rural uses exceeded forecasted demand by 5 per cent; in the fifth year, by 35 per cent. The record for consumption by small nonresidential users, such as the trade and service establishments, was similar— actual use exceeded estimated demand 32 per cent by the fifth year of the forecast.

The Edison Electric Institute's semiannual surveys of future power requirements, compiled from the utilities' own estimates, repeatedly underestimated requirements during the postwar period. Capacity planned to provide adequate reserve margins has proved year after year to be too meager, as loads have exceeded expected growth.

The record of *understating* future power requirements for national defense and for the normal growth of our economy is so consistent and so conclusive that we should carefully re-examine present projections and performance upon which our future welfare and security depend. In 1952 the President's Materials Policy Commission (the Paley Commission) suggested that if total national output should double from 1950 to 1975, as it did during the preceding quarter-century, the demand for electricity would increase three and a half times. Future power requirements of this magnitude—from 389,000,000,000 kilowatt-hours in 1950 to 1,400,000,000,000 kilowatt-hours by 1975— give an impression of phenomenal growth in the national use of electric energy. Yet these very projections assume a rate of growth (260 per cent) considerably below that experienced over the past quarter-century (359 per cent).

6. *National Resources and Foreign Aid: Report of J. A. Krug, U.S. Department of the Interior* (Washington, D.C.: Government Printing Office, 1947), pp. 24–26.

The Paley Commission projections are based broadly on estimated population growth, a rising standard of living for the expanding population, and a doubling of national output. The population estimates used by the commission, however, are now regarded as obsolete. The 1950 Census of Population, which was not available when the commission made its estimates, revealed an unexpected growth in the 1940's. More recent population projections suggest an expected population in 1975 that will exceed by more than ten million the level used by the Paley Commission.[7] Thus the number of new consumers needs to be increased in our calculations.

Another important assumption needs to be re-examined: the question of use per consuming unit. The Paley Commission uses the 1950 national average of 1,900 kilowatt-hours for residential and domestic consumers; it then assumes for its residential and domestic projections that the average will increase to 5,000 by 1975, that is, from 1,900 to 5,000 *in twenty-five years*. In the Tennessee Valley we passed the 1,900-kilowatt-hour average in 1946; the 1975 forecast for the nation— the 5,000-kilowatt-hour figure—is upon us now. It took only eight years for the region to approach the average projected for the nation in 1975 by the Paley Commission.

In the industrial field the Paley Commission assumes that the 6.27 kilowatt-hours used per man-hour in manufacturing (1950) nationally would be increased to 18 kilowatt-hours per man-hour by 1975. This is only a little larger than the rise from 8 to 18 kilowatt-hours per man-hour in manufacturing industries in the Tennessee Valley, and this rise did not require a quarter of a century to be recorded. In the Tennessee Valley the rise from 8 to 18 kilowatt-hours came *in less than a dozen years* (1941–52). And it is important to note that these figures do not include TVA's supply of very large blocks of power to the AEC, the Air Force Wind Tunnel, and other federal defense agencies whose demands added enormously to the power requirements of the region.

These comparisons between actual experience in the Tennessee

7. *Illustrative Projections of the Population of the United States, by Age and Sex: 1955 to 1975* (Bureau of the Census, Series P-25, No. 78 [Washington, D.C., August 21, 1953]), p. 5.

Valley and the assumptions used in the Paley Commission's projections are not intended to suggest that an expansion in the use of electric energy *nationally* will occur at the rate experienced in the Tennessee Valley. In the Tennessee Valley there are a hundred and fifty locally owned municipal and rural electric co-operatives distributing TVA power, jointly pledged, with TVA, to achieve the widest possible distribution at the lowest possible cost. This public enterprise partnership is a unique arrangement getting unique results. The comparisons, however, do suggest a rate of growth which it might be possible to approach nationally, if there were in prospect an adequate national supply of electric energy and an enterprising spirit dedicated to the broadest distribution of electricity at the lowest possible rates.

The Record of Meeting Potential Demand

Planning for the future supply of a service that is so essential to both economic development and the defense of our nation should be imaginative and comprehensive. No one knows how much more the use of power would have exceeded the utility industry's estimate if the supply had been larger and its use encouraged by more enterprising leadership. But the record of the past clearly reveals the electric-power industry's failure to promote the use of electricity during much of the entire period since the commercial introduction of electricity in the United States.

The record of the private utility industry in its plans—or lack of plans—to promote, and then meet, new market demands is illustrated in the early history of rural electrification, in the promotion of electric appliance sales, and, more recently, in its policies with respect to capacity margins.

Rural electrification.—As early as 1910 there were in the United States a few examples of line extensions by private utilities into rural territory, in most instances "showcase" country estates. By 1924 the number of farms with central service had risen to 166,000, according to the electric utility industry's own figures. Electrified farms were less than 3 per cent of all farms. In eighteen states, including all or nearly all of the southern states, the ratio was less than 1 per cent. In Georgia the percentage of farms with central service in 1924—only a generation ago—was one-twentieth of 1 per cent.

In contrast, the progress up to 1923 of rural electrification in other parts of the world can be cited as follows: in Bavaria, 50 per cent of farms with electric service; in Denmark, also about 50 per cent; in Sweden, 40 per cent; in the Province of Ontario, Canada, 80 per cent of the population were served, with a higher ratio of customers in rural than in urban areas. In all these areas except Denmark the government had supplied vigorous initiative to proper electric distribution. However, it is also significant that private power companies had important systems in all areas except Ontario. Extensive rural electrification was considered good business long ago by private power companies *outside* the United States.

In 1935 the Rural Electrification Administration was established in this country to aid rural areas in their quest for electricity. At that time the electric industry in the United States had not yet carried electric service to more than one farm out of eight. The need for introducing more enterprise in this field was obvious.

The main barriers to extension of electric power to farms in the United States before 1935 rested on two rather firmly intrenched policies of the electric companies. One was a rate policy which failed to take into account the potentialities of the rural load. Urban domestic use at the time included little more than electric lights and a few household appliances; farm use of electric energy for motors and machines was priced out of the market by electric rates which assumed electricity was useful mostly for a few light bulbs. Morris L. Cooke, the first administrator of the REA, referring to the period from 1914 to 1936, stated: "Rural rates of from twenty to thirty cents per kilowatt hour were not exceptional, and this on top of the fact that the rural customer almost invariably paid the entire cost of building his extension."[8]

8. "The Early Days of the Rural Electrification Idea: 1914–1936," *American Political Science Review*, XLII (June, 1948), 439.

A second barrier that blocked electric service to farms was the "cream-skimming policy" of the utilities. As early as 1914, in the famous Philadelphia Electric Case, the Pennsylvania Public Service Commission specified that a company operating in a rural area must extend its lines when there was at least one contracting consumer per mile. This specification, however, was not widely adopted. Rural lines, such as they were, continued to probe only into the most lucrative service areas close to the cities.

The development of rural electric service on an area-wide basis had to wait more than twenty years. Then the rural electric co-operative, pioneered in the Tennessee Valley, began to spread widely over the country with the aid of loans from the REA. It revolutionized electric service in rural America. It was the answer to an attitude expressed cogently by the president of a large midwestern privately owned utility: "This is indeed an unusual situation. The farmer, a user of power, is trying to force the utility, a seller of power, to sell him the product it has for sale."[9]

With such a record it is understandable why George M. Gadsby, as the president of the Edison Electric Institute in 1952, was reported as confessing in a moment of candor:

Once, he said, there was an era of good feeling about private power, but back around the '20's, the industry lost its standing. Financial pyramiding and collapse of the holding companies started the down-trend, he pointed out. Delays and impolitic procedures in rural electrification accelerated the process, he said.

"There never would have been the need," he said, "for rural electric co-operatives—and there was a need for them—if private utilities had had more faith in themselves to develop the farm market."[10]

Encouraging new uses.—Had Mr. Gadsby wished, he could have broadened this self-criticism with equal justification to include the

9. Marquis Childs, *The Farmer Takes a Hand* (Garden City, N.Y.: Doubleday & Co., 1952), p. 39. Statement made by Grover Neff, president of Wisconsin Power Company.

10. "It's the People Who Will Decide," *Electrical World*, CXXXVII (May 19, 1952), 122.

industry's failure to be a pioneer in discovering and promoting residential, commercial, and industrial, as well as farm, uses of electricity. The restricted vision of possible household applications of energy was second only to the rural electricity policy. The need for research in new domestic and farm uses of electricity was noted in some of the industry's early literature, but little was accomplished. In 1927, for example, nearly half a century after the commercial introduction of electricity, an industry spokesman commented about retarded use of the electric range:

It cannot be said that the electrical industry has done a good job with respect to poularizing the use of the electric range. . . . This is undoubtedly due to a fear on the part of utility managers that the range load will swamp distribution lines and generating stations and is therefore undesirable.[11]

What does this mean? Simply that the utility industry was reluctant to expand production of electricity, and consequently the promotion of electrical appliances ran into a stone wall. Similar notes were struck by manufacturers of electrical appliances. Addressing the electric utilities, a General Electric Company executive explained: "The [electrical equipment] manufacturer's ability to build up the power company's load . . . is limited by the policies of the power company in every community."[12] Identical attitudes on the part of power companies prevailed—and in some areas still prevail—with respect to electric water heaters and other appliances.

Evidences of this lack of enterprise prevail today. In many areas of the country what was true of the twenties and thirties with respect to electric ranges and water heaters is currently true of electric space heating—heating homes—and other contributions to improved living conditions in the household.

In spite of the tugging by consumers and the prodding by appliance manufacturers, sales in the home and on the farm were relatively insignificant until stimulated by promotional rate policies—where rates

11. H. B. Whiteman, "The Domestic Electric Range," *N.E.L.A. Bulletin*, XIV (March, 1927), 174.

12. A. K. Baylor, "The Manufacturer's Part in Increasing Kilowatt Hour Consumption," *N.E.L.A. Bulletin*, XIV (March, 1927), 151.

are lower per kilowatt-hour when the customer uses more. And here it is important to note that, with a few exceptions, the load-building effectiveness of lower rates had to be demonstrated to the industry by publicly owned systems.

Providing capacity for load growth.—The electric utility industry has a similar record of selling the future short with respect to maintenance of adequate reserve capacity. When in 1942 a writer in the *Public Utilities Fortnightly* suggested that the federal government assist in overcoming the critical power shortage then looming, even at a risk to private "enterprise," we were engaged in war. Under those circumstances the following comment in that journal seems charitable indeed:

It is unfair and perhaps futile to try to assess the blame for inadequate planning of production capacity on any American industry in view of the hectic circumstances of the past year which have caused us to "raise our sights" of armament production, military and naval organization and supply, time and time again.[13]

In 1947, five years later, after the nation demobilized its war strength, it is interesting to hear the president of the Edison Electric Institute speak in terms strikingly reminiscent of the days of wartime shortages. However, he concluded on the optimistic note:

It is evident that the problems of adequate generating capacity arising from rapid load expansion are well on the way to solution. The worries of operating with small reserves of generating capacity which have been ours since last August will begin to diminish in about 7 months, although another 12 months may elapse before they disappear in all parts of the country.[14]

When those seven months had gone by, the situation was reviewed again by an industry spokesman. He adjusted the seven months to two or three years in the following terms: "I think it can be stated as a fact that barring some major disruptions in our industrial operations . . . the power situation will come into a completely normal position

13. Bratter, *op. cit.*, p. 400.

14. G. C. Neff, "The President's Report," *Edison Electric Institute Bulletin*, XV (June, 1947), 194.

by 1950 in most of the country and by 1951 in the entire country."[15]

But, when 1951 arrived, Mr. Sutton, making the presidential address before the Edison Electric Institute, stated:

Our committee reports that this coming December and in December, 1952, we may expect to have about the same percentage of reserve capacity that we had in December, 1950, which was 10 percent. . . . It is about half of what we expected to have before Korea, but on account of the time required to build new generating capacity, the construction program could not be increased in 1950 and 1951, and not until 1953 and 1954 could we expect to gain much increased capability.[16]

Each year, year by year with monotonous regularity during the past dozen years, the theme that adequate reserves to eliminate power shortages would come in another year or two has dominated the industry's pronouncements on power supply. Yet with equal regularity the date by which adequate reserves could be anticipated has been advanced as each new year brought demands to levels unanticipated by power forecasts.

The evidence in figures of performance related to prediction is clear. It is a fact, whether in war or in peace, that, when the nation seeks to operate at a high level of economic activity to expand production consistent with the growing well-being of an expanding population, power supply is found to be inadequate. Unless a more vigorous and practical approach to the question of power supply is adopted, we, as a nation of one hundred and sixty million people, will continue to be penalized by the threat or reality of power shortages.

We have noted the inadequacy of the industry's forecasts, its failure to provide ample capacity, and its unwillingness to build up the loads that could be served if its capacity were increased more rapidly. We can only speculate about how much more electricity the homes,

15. "How Tight Is the Nation's Power Supply?" *Public Utilities Fortnightly*, XLI (January 15, 1948), 113. Statement made by Philip Sporn, president of American Gas & Electric Service Corporation.

16. L. V. Sutton, "The President's Address," *Edison Electric Institute Bulletin*, XIX (July, 1951), 207.

farms, and factories of America would be using if more power had been available. We can only guess how much a greater margin of electric supply would have enhanced our national security.

But we can inform our conjectures by an appeal to actual experience. The Tennessee Valley is one of the few places where power supply has been increased rapidly enough in the last twenty years to lead some industry spokesmen to assert from time to time that a wasteful surplus was being created. The demands for power continue to surpass even our much-criticized forecasts. Today in the Tennessee Valley the average home uses nearly twice as much electricity as in the rest of the country. The electricity consumers of the Tennessee Valley buy more than $100 million of new appliances each year, creating a billion-dollar market since the close of World War II. Total home and farm uses are nearly *forty times* the consumption of power for those uses twenty years ago. Total consumption per capita runs almost as high in the Tennessee Valley as in a leading electrified nation such as Norway, almost double the United States average. Industrial and commercial loads represent a fifteen-fold expansion over similar loads in 1933. A large part, almost three-quarters, of the commercial and industrial load represents use directly related to the national defense. Atomic-energy operations, aluminum for aircraft, the guided missile and aircraft testing programs, and other federal defense production and operations absorb more than half of the total output of the TVA system, the largest single integrated power system in the country. And by 1956, when the system will be twice as large as it is now, atomic-energy operations alone at Paducah, Kentucky, and Oak Ridge, Tennessee, will take one-half of all the energy the Authority will generate.

What explains this phenomenal growth of power use in the Tennessee Valley? The region's power agencies have an abiding faith that a democratic community, possessing the will and spirit of enterprise to use its resources wisely and fully, has capacity to grow far beyond today's carefully calculated prediction. The Tennessee Valley has seen electricity work as an ingredient, a positive force, whose very availability will stimulate inventive use of energy and thus continue the elasticity of demand for it.

The experience of the Tennessee Valley and other examples of public power development in the United States contain valuable lessons for those who are prepared to face facts about this country's inadequate power supply.

The Problem Today

The record of the past indicates the seriousness of the power-supply problem that the nation continues to face. An ample power supply in fact and for future prospects can be a positive force for economic growth. Constant underbuilding of new capacity is an impediment to our development. The electric utility industry therefore must foresee and provide for power expansion well ahead of rapidly growing demand. The failure of the industry to do so in the early years of its history may in part be explained by a lack of experience and knowledge characteristic of new industries. But such reasons cannot be accepted for the performance during the last ten or fifteen years.

The general problem of making the electric utility industry a positive force for continued national expansion involves both an adequate physical supply and a minimum level of cost. It has often been argued that "some claims of power shortage . . . have proved to be merely an unwillingness to pay the rate necessary to purchase a needed power supply."[17] This suggests that, under monopoly service, *demand* need only be controlled at any level by pricing some would-be users out of the market. Such an attitude is inexcusable when it is possible to have an adequate supply at lower costs through more enterprising behavior. Certainly we all recognize, for example, the need to conduct our national defense with a minimum drain on manpower and materials.

An unnecessarily high cost for power due to an inadequate rate of power expansion is a problem not limited to wartime. Power rates that are higher than they need to be have exerted a retarding influence on the expansion of the nation over the last decade and longer, owing

17. C. W. Kellogg, "The President's Address," *op. cit.*, p. 222.

to the industry's failure to maintain adequate margins of reserve. With inadequate generating capacity to meet the peak loads and maintain reserve capacity, the industry has continued to operate aged and obsolete facilities at excessive costs. The use of obsolete facilities is not a rare and unusual situation. In fact, a quarter of the nation's thermal electric-power capacity—steam electric units—was installed more than twenty-five years ago.

Lack of an adequate power supply makes power cost more. This keeps rates high. And high rates slow down the expansion of a dynamic free-enterprise economy. The effects operate in a vicious cycle. The slower growth in power use itself discourages a rapid shift in the power industry to modern low-cost generating facilities, and this in turn restricts consumption.

The failure to provide a supply of power adequate for the nation's economic growth is a serious, though not fatal, problem. But failure to provide a supply of power adequate for defense contingencies is a security risk we cannot afford to take, for, unlike other critical defense materials, electrical energy, as distinguished from the capacity to generate electricity, cannot be stockpiled.

The technology and logistics of power supply are different from most commercial enterprises. Compared with the heavy and durable goods industries, such as steel, aluminum, and automobiles, the generating end of the electric industry has special problems of time and the ratio of investment to earnings. It is important that these differences be understood. Unlike the construction of many other types of production facilities which can be expanded in a matter of months, the construction of power-generating capacity must begin well in advance of the demand for power. Electrical generation and transmission has become a highly complex industry. The constant drive for greater efficiency in generating units to get more kilowatt-hours from a unit of heat (coal, oil, or gas) suggests continuous revision of designs.

Twelve or fifteen years ago the 25,000-kilowatt steam electric unit was considered rather large; today TVA is installing steam units of 250,000-kilowatt capacity, the largest in the history of the industry. Technology is advancing so rapidly that most steam-generator units are custom built to these changing designs. Consequently, about four years are now required to plan, finance, design, and place a large modern steam plant in operation. And even longer periods may be required for the larger hydropower facilities.

In contrast, plants to produce defense materials which require large quantities of electricity per ton of product, such as aluminum and titanium, can be built within a year. Therefore, unless a reservoir of uncommitted power capacity is available, three years could elapse before a newly expanded defense requirement is energized economically, if at all. During the past war, for example, a large amount of aluminum ingot capacity had to be located in areas where power costs were high because of shortages of power capacity in areas where power costs are low. The federal government, buying airplanes, paid for these high power rates in the cost of aluminum. A widespread use of "cost-plus" contracts between the government and the producer in this circle of wartime procurement pyramided high power costs in the final product. The individual citizen paid for this high-cost power in higher taxes to pay for the cost of the bomber; when the plants built in wartime in areas of high-cost power could not be operated economically in peacetime, the plants were sold or scrapped with a large loss in the government's investment. This loss fell on the taxpayer. As one example, $86 million invested in more than a third of a million tons of modern efficient aluminum capacity had to be scrapped after World War II because power costs were too high for these plants to compete in a peacetime market. Only a few years later, during the Korean War, new aluminum capacity had to be built again.

During the Korean War period, as during World War II, however, a part of the nation's aluminum was produced with unnecessarily high power costs because power supply was inadequate. The cost to the taxpayers is measured in millions of dollars in the cost of bombers. To these costs should be added the reduced corporate income taxes under tax-amortization certificates which were issued to private utilities to get them to build the capacity required. A shortage of power is costly in other ways; while waiting for new generating capacity to be built, the Atomic Energy Commission has paid many millions of dollars of excess power costs because the only power available had to be taken from small, high-cost power plants and transmitted long distances at great expense. These unnecessary costs to the taxpayer are a direct result of an inadequate supply of economically produced power. These circumstances restrain economic progress; they are a source of weakness in our nation's defense.

The unanticipated use of electric energy for purposes not yet conceived, just as the need for power to make atomic weapons or more aluminum was not foreseen, is an equally important justification for creating defense power reserves. If the Edison Electric Institute's claim had been believed—that the "power situation will be found to have been adequately provided for"[18] (expressed by its president, Mr. Kellogg, when serving in the federal government in 1941)—construction of the proposed dams then under discussion would not have been begun. Two years later, when Oak Ridge was ready, power would not have been available. The atom bomb would not have been ready on that fateful day over Japan. For it took longer to build new power supply than was required to build Oak Ridge; TVA's head start, its insistent preparation for the unexpected, underscores the vital importance of farsighted preparedness in power supply in planning for national strength.

In the next chapter we shall go further in trying to understand why the past record of the private utilities has been less than satisfactory; we shall describe a course of action that should help them measure up to their responsibilities. To repeat what a former chairman of the Authority said, "The time for nibbling cautiously at power supply is long since past."

18. *Ibid.*

VI. National Power Policy

Introduction

In our discussion of power—of electricity—it is important that our minds be clear on one point: electricity is not just another "commercial product" to be placed on the commodity market at the highest price it will bring. Electric energy is a basic necessity of community and national life, an absolute requirement for national strength and security.

In the preceding chapter I dipped into the history of the electric utility industry to show how its record of power capacity expansion has failed to recognize the vital role electric energy should play in our economic life.

In this chapter we shall try to understand why the utility industry has turned in a record of performance somewhat less than "brilliant," even less than "satisfactory." Some of the reasons tend to absolve the industry of blame, but one cannot excuse it for its failure to discharge the responsibility it has sought and accepted from the public—the electricity consumers and the public bodies that grant it franchise and monopoly privileges. As we try to find out why the past record leaves much to be desired, we shall seek clues to constructive suggestions for improved performance in the future.

What has been said thus far on the subject of electric power should make it clear that I would not propose public ownership of the electric utility industry as the solution to our problem of an ample energy supply for the nation. Nor would I agree that the answer will be found by eliminating, neutralizing, or crippling the publicly owned power systems now in operation or in resistance to further public power development on the ground of abstract ideologies. The question of who owns our power systems *is* secondary to the question of *ample* power supply.

Is the Power Supply Problem Being Solved?

The continuing inadequate margins to which spokesmen of the utility industry testify and the excessive costs which a power shortage creates have two serious implications for the future of the nation. These conditions hinder the growth of our economy and the drive for more efficient, lower-cost production of the things we use. What is worse, an inadequate power supply involves risks to the nation's security. How are these problems being solved?

The chronic inadequacy of power supply is conclusive evidence that most of the electrical industry has not yet perceived the problem, much less taken effective action to solve it. Every year in which the industry spokesmen have admitted the inadequacy of power reserve margins they have reassured their customers and themselves that power aplenty is just ahead. The phrase "tight power supply" continues to be an accurate description, however, despite the annual prediction of forthcoming adequate reserves.

When the United Nations grasped the nettle of a world-wide issue in Korea, it was evident that there was no margin of power supply to absorb the effect of mobilization. Nor was it certain that the industry was willing and able to finance all the new capacity that was needed. The industry was therefore granted access to tax-amortization certificates. Many million kilowatts of capacity have been covered by these interest-free loans granted through tax relief.

Presumably by now, after some months of truce in Korea, the nation should have an ample margin of power supply. Where is it? With some dip in industrial production at the end of 1953, some will say that finally an ample margin existed. The fact is that there was no real margin at all. *During the fall of 1953 the total amount of spare power purchasable from the great industrial area between the Great Lakes and the Tennessee Valley was not enough to supply the power-consuming capacity of aluminum and atomic-energy production.* As a result these important plants had to reduce the scale of their operations, and part of their facilities stood idle. The price of such limited power as was available was judged to be too high for the defense program to pay.

If we had been conducting an all-out war, cost would have been secondary; but dollars in the till are no substitute for power when the power cannot be produced. In an emergency it is commonplace for the uninformed to suggest that rationing of power will provide what we need for defense. The experience of this country in World War II showed that even the most heroic efforts to extract a margin of power from the curtailment of civilian uses cannot recapture large amounts when or where they are needed. Electricity, unlike butter, has no substitute.

Why Does the Power Supply Problem Persist?

An adequate power supply for the nation is a crucial problem which vitally affects the nation's welfare. But, in order to take effective public action, we must understand the reasons behind the failure of the electric utility industry to fulfil its responsibility.

Is the failure to anticipate the nation's power needs merely a result of poor guessing? Forecasts dealing with the behavior of variables are always difficult to make. Random factors outside the scope of the forecasters' accountability will always produce deviations from actual future results. But careful and intelligent forecasting will err in both directions—above and below actual demands that develop.

If forecasts are consistently biased in one direction—and they are nearly always too low—there must be relevant factors that are being consistently overlooked. The electric utility industry, which has its exclusive franchise and public utility privileges, has an obligation to identify all the demand factors and include them in its plans for future capacity. Nothing short of this is consistent with the public responsibility that an enterprise must accept to justify a monopoly franchise.

What, then, are the factors which are not fully considered? The record suggests two very important answers: (1) the effect of new or potential uses of electricity is not taken into account and (2) there is a "built-in" psychological conservatism on the part of forecasters who evaluate the market for products of high-investment industries, that is, industries which require a large investment per unit of revenue.

If the market for a product is approaching saturation, the growth curve bends over. If new uses are continually developing, the growth curve rises more and more steeply, For many years the growth of power use has trended upward sharply, but the industry, year after year, has projected a curve reflecting a loss of momentum in its upward drive. Pinned down, the forecasters admit a hesitation to allow for the new uses that cannot be named in advance but always develop.

Equally, if not more, important is the understandable propensity of the industry to keep capacity reserves at a minimum. Idle capacity could be a costly affair because of the extremely high ratio of investment to revenue. The industry may also fear that any expansion of capacity for which loads are not ready and waiting might be viewed by the regulatory commissions as not representing "prudent investment" on which a return should be provided in the electric rate approved. And low rate of return jeopardizes credit.

It would be cavalier to leave the impression that all utility managements have a blind spot on the subject of expansion requirements. I have heard utility executives in private conversations speak of the need for a greater rate of expansion in terms not much less emphatic than those which I have used. It is most unfortunate that so few will say the same in public. Even a progressive utility management is not in a position to add to its capacity as fast as it would like. The financial markets keep close watch on the debt, interest, and dividend records of individual companies. The money markets do not reward risk-taking in the utility business. Some of the least progressive utilities, those with low average consumer use and very high rates, may through their conservatism have earned the coveted A-1 financial rating which makes them welcome when they come to the market place for new capital—even though they come too late for too little. Some of the most farsighted and aggressive companies, eager to anticipate the needs of the areas they serve, may for that very reason be required to pay a higher rate of interest or dividends for the money which is lent or subscribed. The tremendous capital requirements for electric service are thus a heavy drag on the expansion of the electric utilities, and most of all upon those which try to do the best job of preparing to serve their present and future loads.

The result of serving new or expanding loads with inadequate capacity is even more costly than carrying a surplus. The tendency to limit reserve margins, added to the failure to include the full range of relevant considerations in estimating the demand for power, results in too little capacity and too much obsolete capacity for economic operations.

This tendency is related to another and major basic factor underlying our present power shortage situation: I refer to the monopoly structure of the electric utility industry. Its status as a monopoly is intended to be offset to some extent by public regulation. Public regulation can protect the consumer against overt exploitation, but the regulatory commission at its very best is a poor substitute for competition. Regulation, as the word suggests, is a process of saying "No" or "You can't do that." Regulation cannot assume the positive responsibilities of management to press for reduced costs and higher efficiency. Regulation has *not* created the necessary incentives to provide adequate service and to reduce cost and price through aggressive development of greater use of electricity. The lack of direct competition fosters a management of complacency bred by a cost-plus security paid for by the consumer, who cannot shop around in buying his electricity. Management under these circumstances gets lazy and is incapable of the type of enterprising behavior which characterizes competitive situations.

The *Electrical World*, in an editorial, expressed it this way:

In a competitive business there is the same eagerness to secure a fair return on invested capital, but the approach is different. Return in a competitive business comes from expansion in sales—from volume. . . .

In a competitive business one does not start with a rate that will produce a return and struggle to build business at that price. Just the opposite; one sets a goal and then finds out what price is necessary to reach that figure. The costs are adjusted to make that price bring a return on the estimated volume.

What is the difference? Just this, that growth under the monopolistic concept is necessarily slower than under the competitive concept. Rates in one case are protective of investment, while on the other they are volume creative.[1]

The Spur of Competition

Fortunately, there has been some competition in the electric-power industry. I refer, of course, to the division of the industry between public and private ownership. To illustrate the effect of competition, it is necessary only to examine the behavior of the utility industry in the areas surrounding the Tennessee Valley. *Business Week*, speaking of the chairman of the board of Arkansas Power and Light Company, says: "Ham Moses has been afraid of something like an Arkansas TVA for 20 years. He has fought it by pushing rural electrification, by selling power to rural cooperatives cheaper than the Government's power systems could, and by building Arkansas."[2] The Tennessee Valley Authority is complimented by such aggressive preventive emulation.

Competition is not a one-way street. Many of the publicly owned systems, together with the rural co-operatives, feel the stimulus of competition most keenly.

We are a people with a profound conviction in the efficacy of competitive enterprise. In specific instances we sometimes forget that private ownership is not synonymous with competitive enterprise. Public ownershp is frequently met by strong opposition. The privately owned systems trade upon their claimed synonymity with competitive enterprise to win public support; they carry the fight to advocates of public ownership by invoking a charge of "socialism." The publicly owned systems plead comparative performance as the basis for a fair verdict, and the tonic of competition begins its salutary work. Areas of public ownership have been subjected continuously to the scrutiny

1. CXIX (June 26, 1943), 2111.
2. May 30, 1953, p. 84.

of their critics. Such public attention has frequently helped morale and impelled the highest standard of performance from the public power systems; pride of competence and a desire to excel in a service imbued with a dedication to the public interest sometimes reach their highest pitch under fire. Competition can do no more!

The public systems have done the best job where there has been the greatest drive for widespread use of electricity combined with the strongest contest from the private utilities. In those areas we have an opportunity to judge the effect of competition.

The whole world is becoming familiar with the examples of public power operations in the Tennessee Valley and in the Pacific Northwest, with the great installations of power capacity that have taken place in those two areas. Both areas show an unusually rapid growth in power use, lower rates, and a sound financial result.

In the last twenty years the Authority, operating as a producer and transmitter of power, the least lucrative part of the utility business, has earned an average rate of return of more than 4 per cent on the net average investment in power facilities. This return is what is left after paying all costs of operation, depreciation, and payments in lieu of taxes to state and local governments. This return more than covers the cost of money to the government, that is, interest, and leaves a tidy dividend besides. Out of power revenues TVA is paying back, over a forty-year period, all appropriated funds invested in power properties. Payments thus far are well ahead of schedule.

A typical privately owned utility not only generates and transmits power in bulk but distributes it to the retail consumer. But in the Tennessee Valley the distribution facilities that carry electricity from delivery points to more than one million, three hundred thousand retail consumers are owned by the public distributors—the cities, towns, and rural co-operatives. The annual rate of return on the net investment for these distribution systems averages about 8 per cent.

What has been the effect of public power operations upon the surrounding privately owned utilities?

The competitive example public power creates is analyzed by the

President's Water Resources Policy Commission studies published in 1950. These studies reveal that in areas in which a federal agency is actively marketing power from river-basin developments the cost of power purchased by rural co-operatives from near-by *private companies* is about half as high as the cost of similar power where no competitive forces are in operation.

To quote from the Commission's report:

> One can compare the southeastern states (South Carolina, Georgia, Alabama, and Mississippi) with the northeastern states having rural electric co-operatives (Maine, New Hampshire, Vermont, New York, and Pennsylvania). The first region has been profoundly affected by the TVA and to a lesser extent by the South Carolina Public Service Authority. The second has had no such influence. Both have water power resources.[3]

Wholesale rates to co-operatives in the private utility areas surrounding TVA average about three-quarters of a cent, whereas in the Northeast the average rate runs nearly twice as high. In fact, when a series of concentric zones moving outward from the Tennessee Valley power service area and the Pacific Northwest is shown on a map of the United States and in those zones the average wholesale electric rates charged to the rural co-operatives are recorded, the results strikingly portray the wholesome effects of competition (Fig. 2). One sees successively higher charges as one moves farther and farther from the Northwest and the Tennessee Valley, the two major centers of competition between public and private power.

I should emphasize at this point that inherently lower-cost sources of power cannot be advanced as the governing factor in these rate differentials. The zone comparisons I have described persist even when adjusted to equalize differences in fuel costs.

A similar comparison may be made for residential rates. In 1933, when private utilities operated in the Tennessee Valley, average rates for residential use were among the highest to be found in any region in the country. And those rates had not been substantially changed for

3. President's Water Resources Policy Commission, *A Water Policy for the American People* (Washington, D.C.: Government Printing Office, 1950), I, 229.

years. Today the Tennessee Valley ranks with the Northwest in having the lowest rates for residential use. And now the residential rates charged by private utilities adjacent to this service area are substantially below the rates charged in the North, in the East, and in the Middle West.

The companies operating around the Tennessee Valley have profited in other ways from TVA's example. In 1933, soon after the creation of the Authority, the Georgia and Alabama power companies

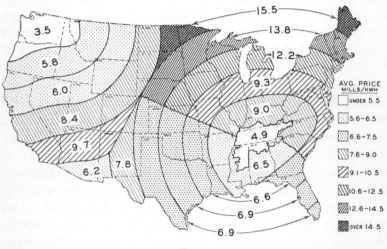

FIG. 2

found a new way to stimulate customer use by a promotional rate which offered a discount for higher use. Since 1933 these companies have promoted greater use of electricity. They have competed vigorously with the Rural Electrification Administration co-operatives for rural loads, especially in the more densely settled rural areas. When co-operatives began to talk about building generating plants to reduce wholesale costs, the private companies offered power at wholesale on terms low enough to keep the business. And in those towns and rural areas immediately adjacent to the Authority's operations, service and cultivation of consumer goodwill form a veritable wall—the best way in the world for the private companies to prevent consumers from pleading for TVA electricity!

What has happened to the rate of power-capacity expansion in those private utility areas nearest the Tennessee Valley? Has the threat of a public power neighbor, expanding its power capacity about 500 per cent since 1933, scared capital away and frozen the neighboring private utility systems into static paralysis? Not at all! On the contrary, low-rate policies and inspired merchandising in the Tennessee Valley public power systems have resulted in a notable expansion by neighboring private utilities. Note these comparative figures: The expansion of power-generating plants for the nation has been less than 150 per cent since 1933; if the national figures are limited to privately owned systems and adjusted to exclude the private-company neighbors of the Authority, we find an increase between 1933 and 1952 of only 91 per cent. But in the eight states adjacent to Tennessee[4] (exclusive of TVA's capacity in some of these states) power capacity owned by private utilities has increased 200 per cent since 1933 when the Act was passed!

In the six New England States where the private utilities are at a safe distance from any effective competition from federal power developments a fact that suggests one of the reasons why the inviting power potential of the St. Lawrence has been so long delayed the level of power rates is highest and growth of power supply has been slowest. Power capacity in New England has increased only 75 per cent compared with the national increase of 150 per cent and the increase of 200 per cent among the private companies adjoining TVA.

These recitals make it clear that competition between public and private power has benefited the consumer of electric energy. The competition from public power projects brought reduction of rates and expansion of capacity and service in areas served by private utilities. How about the stockholders of the private companies who have "suffered," as they say, from the competitive proximity of public

4. These states include Arkansas, Alabama, Georgia, Kentucky, Mississippi, North and South Carolina, and Virginia.

power enterprise? Federal Power Commission data show that financial returns have been excellent for those private utilities stirred by neighboring, if not neighborly, public enterprise. TVA's neighbors are making more money now than they did before the Authority began to worry them. Composite rates of return for all Class A and B electric utilities in the United States, when compared with electric utilities operating in areas adjoining the Valley and the public power area of the Northwest, reveal that stockholders have not been adversely affected by the policy of rate competition and expansion of service. In fact, average earnings among private companies in areas adjoining these public power operations have exceeded the national average.

The experience of private utilities adjacent to TVA is very illuminating on this point. The common-stock earnings of major privately owned utilities contiguous to this public power (with 1937–39 as a base of 100) moved to 275 in 1946, while the comparable United States total reached 137. By 1952 the earnings of these private utility neighbors moved to 510 on the index, while the comparable United States total reached 225. Thus the dollar profits of the private owners of power systems over the nation are twice as large as fifteen years ago; but the private company neighbors of TVA are enjoying profits five times as large as they were before demonstration of this public enterprise began to prod them into action.

The excellent financial results shown by the Authority's neighbors have come not in spite of but because of lowered rates which are below former levels and below national averages. Use per consuming unit has gone up, generating capacity has been expanded more rapidly with improved efficiency in production costs per kilowatt-hour, and more kilowatt-hours sold have spread overheads over a larger volume.

The irony of this situation should be apparent. Most utilities would show better earnings if they performed a better public service. Instead of opposing TVA with political slogans and economic dogma, they might prudently foster a warm espousal of a few aggressive centers of public power examples in their midst. Let them accept and encourage the meaning of the word "enterprise" which they so expensively advertise. The further development of the Columbia River's great power resources marketed by public managers, the development and use of the St. Lawrence and Niagara and Missouri under public auspices, the addition of steam-generating plants in the hands of federations of rural electric co-operatives, and the continued expansion of hydro and steam facilities in the Tennessee Valley by the Authority will help to keep alive and make more alert an otherwise complacent monopoly industry.

Competition benefits the consumer and the nation. And the record shows competition brings the private companies' stockholders a higher dividend. What a challenge to a real spirit of enterprise!

What Other Methods Should Be Used?

If the privately owned utilities are reluctant to expand rapidly because of a possible risk to their investors from having surplus capacity, or because of a too cautious attitude in the money market, let us find a way to help them. Competition from public power enterprises is one way—it is the best way—a minimum plank in any national power policy that makes sense. But there may be additional devices to be considered.

Do the private electric utilities want assistance? The record shows they are not reluctant in seeking outside aid. The response of the private utilities to the rapid tax-amortization privileges offered by the federal government as an inducement to strengthen defense production shows the eagerness of the industry to receive help. This arrangement, in effect, makes interest-free loans from the United States Treasury to private corporations by allowing depreciation of physical assets covered by tax certificates to be calculated on a five-year basis instead of the full useful life of the new asset. In each year one-fifth of the investment, instead of one-thirtieth or one-fortieth is deducted from earnings to arrive at the figure on which federal corporate income tax is paid. This device, available by federal law and enacted when the Korean War started, was designed to encourage private business firms to build facilities for national defense which might be considered marginal by ordinary investment standards.

As of June, 1953, according to the Defense Electric Power Administration, 636 electric-power projects have received certificates for rapid tax amortization. These projects are increasing United States electric-power capacity by some 22,000,000 kilowatts over about a three-year period. Note these figures carefully, because three years is about what it takes to build generating plants. Twenty-two million kilowatts of new capacity is about equal to the 1950–53 expansion program of all utilities; if we are to assume that this expansion, consistent with the purpose of the tax-amortization scheme, would not have been undertaken by the utilities without federal assistance, it would follow that the lack of enterprise and the fear of surplus power capacity among utilities are even more serious than I have contended.

There is a more important inference to be drawn from the facts of this situation: The present expansion program for new power capacity will do little more than meet normal civilian demands under conditions of economic expansion. Some power margins will appear if industrial expansion stops or if we go into a depression. But nowhere in the program for future power supply can be found a pool of reserve capacity to meet unpredictable national security needs or the emergencies of a wartime economy. On the contrary, the presently scheduled expansion is being quickly eaten up by the steady growth of nondefense outlets. The tax-amortization policy as applied to present private utility expansion programs thus is being used for purposes other than those for which it was conceived; namely, to underwrite capacity to be used for supposedly temporary national defense loads but presumably surplus to normal requirements.

The assistance sought by the private utilities in financing expansion through the interest-free-loan feature of rapid tax amortization has been helpful in one respect; the eagerness of the utilities to avail themselves of this plan strongly implies that they recognize the drag placed upon expansion by the heavy capital requirements of the power business.

This particular program of federal aid to private utilities, and the industry's willingness to embrace it, admits the problem but is deficient in at least two respects: (1) it is not candid and (2) it does not offer much promise of solving the problem.

Perhaps we should look for an alternative which would protect the investor in private utilities against idle capacity actually earmarked for defense contingencies and, in addition, reduce the risk to investors arising from overexpansion for nondefense requirements. There are a number of ways this could be done. One suggestion is to establish governmental guaranties against losses from surpluses which actually occur. This would be better than giving blanket assistance to cover normal expansion or assuring financial protection in advance against surpluses which are forecast but which never in fact materialize. Such a guaranty, operating in accord with insurance principles, would cost the government nothing if surpluses did not in fact occur. It should help to break down the "built-in" psychological pessimism of the private utilities, which holds back on expansion until demand is assured. The time lag between requirements and capacity in operation to meet those needs could be reduced.

There is another possibility which may be worth serious consideration—one which would cost very little and probably nothing. The federal government might subscribe capital to the utilities in the form of second-preference stock without voting rights. This preferred stock would have a fixed yield lower than required for private investment but high enough to cover the cost of money to the government and a reserve for possible losses. Such an arrangement would help to encourage more private investment for expanding power capacity; a small portion of lower-cost capital would strengthen the yield for the private investors in the company and provide a degree of protection against the risk of overexpansion of power supply.

How much would such a plan of federal aid to private utilities cost? Capital subscriptions by the federal government need cost the taxpayer very little, if anything at all. An insurance scheme to reduce the risk of actual surpluses would be less than the present cost, under tax amortization, of underwriting forecasted surpluses. Either proposal or both, in addition to more competition of the kind I have described, might help to bring power capacity up to the level consistent with the nation's growing needs. This would reduce the incalculable cost arising from impediments to economic growth.

To Meet the Special Needs for National Defense

To meet the special problem of additional reserves adequate for unanticipated national security loads, our defense program should be broadened to provide reservoirs of reserve power in strategic low-cost power areas. Inasmuch as energy cannot be stockpiled, it is imperative to build a special margin of electric-generating capacity to meet unforeseen emergency requirements.

There is no agency, public or private, responsible for taking into account explicitly, and making provisions for, unanticipated large defense loads. This explains why the Atomic Energy Commission, required to increase its activities on short notice because of the international situation, has more than once been compelled to pay more than a million dollars a month in excess charges for power. Obviously, under such circumstances, a prior investment in modern low-cost power capacity would quickly be paid for from the savings.

The excess costs and risks incurred in relation to power supply are avoided largely in other phases of our national security program by arrangements similar to what is suggested here for the electric utility industry. The nation's merchant marine, for example, to be kept in a state of readiness, has in recent times received close to 45 per cent of the domestic costs of vessel construction through governmental assistance—"subsidies," if you will.[5] Approximately a half-billion dollars annually is provided by the federal government to underwrite the merchant fleet and to provide navigation aids and facilities to maintain it in a condition necessary for national security.[6]

In the field of air transport, governmental subsidies similarly help

5. *Editorial Research Reports*, I (February 23, 1950), 142–43. See also *Business Week*, May 24, 1952, p. 31. "In April, 1949, the United States Lines contracted with the Maritime Administration for the construction and purchase of the superliner U[nited] S[tates]. U.S. Lines would pay $28,084,216; the government would pay $18,255,270 in construction differential subsidies plus $24,060,270 to cover national defense features—to make the ship readily convertible into the world's fastest troop carrier" (*Business Week*, June 28, 1952, p. 28).

6. *Editorial Research Reports*, I (February 23, 1950), 143. See also *Congressional Record*, XCVI (March 24, 1950), 4063–64.

to maintain the industry in readiness. The Federal Airport Act of 1946 authorized the expenditure of a half-billion dollars over a seven-year period in grants-in-aid for airports. This, of course, is in addition to the millions of dollars of annual air-mail payments to assist airlines.[7] The Defense Transport Administration of the federal government proposed within recent weeks that the federal government bear a large share of the cost of "mothballing" obsolete rail passenger cars and help to underwrite railroad purchase of new rolling stock, thus establishing a reserve of equipment for emergency use in the future.[8]

One can reserve or pronounce judgment on the wisdom or necessity of each of these programs only as information and reasoning suggest, and I do not cite these examples to indorse or condemn them. But, presumably, these expenditures are made to strengthen the national defense and to eliminate delays and excessive costs caused by general shortages to which the nation would be subjected in the event of war.

To make provision for these features of national defense while ignoring power supply is to cultivate an unwarranted sense of security. Power is vital to national defense, and generating plants take three or four years to build. A reserve of uncommitted power capacity should be built to add to our strength as a measure of preventing war and to permit immediate expansion of energy output in the event war cannot be avoided.

To achieve the greatest economy to the nation, however, the reserve capacity should not be provided indiscriminately by high- and low-cost systems alike, as is the case under the tax-amortization program. The reservoir of defense emergency power should be created in areas where the power systems are able and ready to make the power available at low cost. Defense loads, paid for by the nation's taxpayers, should be supplied at the lowest attainable cost.

These defense reserves, once created, must be held available for

7. *Editorial Research Reports*, I (February 23, 1950), 143, 150. See also Selig Altschul, "Air-Mail Subsidies; Recent Court Rulings May Trim Carriers' Take," *Barron's*, XXXIII (May 25, 1953), 13–14.

8. *New York Times*, January 15, 1954, p. 31.

emergencies. That does not mean they will be idle. The utilities will, of course, use the most economical capacity available to serve their loads. It will be the least economical capacity which is held in standby. The difference in operating costs between the least and most economical capacity will go far toward servicing the additional investment. In effect, I am suggesting a large increase in the proportion of utility reserves and a new conception of their purpose. The availability of large increments of capacity will be a powerful stimulant to general industrial expansion, and at the same time the maintenance of these margins will be a vital element of defense insurance. The additional reserve capacity will entail additional carrying charges, but TVA's experience demonstrates that these carrying charges would be offset in whole or in large measure by the operating economies they make possible.

An increase in the margin of reserves would make it possible to retire the most ancient and expensive of the capacity now held for standby purposes, capacity which is already fully depreciated. Inadequate reserve margins require utilities to use their so-called "teakettle" plants more frequently than they prefer because of their extremely high operating costs. If the utilities could maintain a more adequate margin of reserves, these plants could be junked. Reserves could then consist of capacity within shooting distance of present-day standards of efficiency and economy. These reservoirs of low-cost energy would necessarily be interconnected through flexible transmission systems to shuttle power to areas of shortage during times of war. Until such a power supply is created, adequate and flexible to serve the nation's defense needs, this nation has unwittingly increased the peril in which it lives.

The modest plan of federal aid for private utilities I have suggested, unlike the present rapid amortization scheme, might help to lay the specter that haunts the efforts of private utility executives when they project their financial requirements into the future and begin to build. These suggestions for federal aid to private utilities are not a substitute for competition. The basic feature of our future program should be continued and expanded support for the public power developments already at hand and in prospect. The generating and transmission program sponsored by the Rural Electrification Administration for rural electric co-operative federations should not be curtailed but should proceed unabated, examined case by case, as in the past, and decided on its merits. The continued development of our rivers to harness the latent hydroelectric power along the Missouri, the Columbia, the Snake, and the St. Lawrence should be pressed with new vigor under public auspices, ownership, and operation. The history of the electric business shows a crucial need for the competitive effects of healthy examples of alternative ways of achieving our goal—an ample supply of low-cost power.

Cost Benefits of an Adequate Power Supply

Let us for a moment speculate on the effects of such a national policy. With guaranties against actual losses from idle capacity, private utilities may be stimulated to expand more rapidly. With adequate power on hand, but with no profit underwritten for idle capacity, the utilities might be stimulated to emulate the merchandising job done by TVA and others, where lower rates and smaller margins of price over cost have expanded power consumption enormously.

What might be the effect of such a program on power costs and electric rates?

Expansion of output will require modern, economic capacity, thus reducing the proportion of old and inefficient capacity in the total power supply. In 1951 approximately one-fourth of the total United States steam capacity was more than twenty-five years old; much of it was more than thirty years old. During the past quarter-century rapid technological progress in power generation has significantly reduced generating costs for modern plants. For example, a steam plant of 40,000–60,000 kilowatts can be built today to generate power at a cost 20–25 per cent below the kilowatt-hour cost of twelve years ago. Today's plant uses fuels more efficiently and requires less operating labor. These economies of 25 per cent are in spite of the increase in construction costs in the same period; and with larger units, that is, within a range of 200,000–300,000 kilowatts, generating costs are even lower by 10–15 per cent than for the smaller plants (40,000–60,000 kilowatts).

The economies available in newer and larger-size plants can be shown from TVA's own experience: The Watts Bar Steam Plant, completed in 1945, is a very efficient steam plant judged by the industrial standards and state of the art of today or of ten years ago. It has a rated capacity of 240,000 kilowatts, made up of four units, each rated at 60,000 kilowatts. The Johnsonville Steam Plant, built a few years later, is rated at 675,000 kilowatts, with each of its units about twice as large as the Watts Bar units. Higher boiler pressures, higher temperatures, more capacity in relation to plant-site costs, and other technical factors make the larger units more efficient. A pound of coal produces more electrical energy at Johnsonville than at Watts Bar. Operating expenses are from 15 to 20 per cent lower at the larger plant. These economies have been achieved despite the rise in construction costs since World War II. When modern, efficient, large-scale units are contrasted with plants built long before Watts Bar, the difference in generating costs runs from 30 to 40 per cent or greater.

Economies in distribution costs can also be achieved. Ample supplies of power provide an incentive for promoting wider use of electricity, because distribution costs are reduced with increased volume of sales. Mass sales spread overhead, promotion, and general administrative expenses over a larger volume of production, thereby reducing the unit cost. Larger use per customer reduces distribution costs as well as accounting and collection costs per kilowatt-hour.

Mass-distribution economies explain why the cost per kilowatt-hour of producing, transmitting, distributing, and managing the sale of electricity is about half as large in the Tennessee Valley as in the nation's privately owned utility systems. In the TVA area the cost of producing a kilowatt-hour and delivering it to the ultimate consumer is 5.4 mills—about a half of a cent. The comparable cost for the nation's privately owned utilities in 1952 was 10.1 mills—about twice as much. These are figures unaffected by argument over theories—these are actual direct costs. Both figures are before interest, taxes, and profits.

A quarter (1.2 mills) of the favorable differential in total costs the TVA area enjoys is due to lower costs in customer accounting and collection, sales promotion, and administration. About a fifth of the difference is due to economies in transmission and distribution. And here is a fact that helps to explain these differences: the average use per residential consuming unit in cities of 50,000 population or over in the Tennessee Valley is almost three times as high as the average for the nation's cities of similar size. Greater volume of sales cuts down overhead and fixed charges for each unit sold. No wonder the economies of distribution and administration are substantial!

Conclusion

In view of the record, this is no time to let the nation's power supply turn into a bone of contention. Nor can the federal government calmly step aside and assume somebody—just anybody—will build the power capacity the nation needs. A concern for the national security should counsel caution in neutralizing or destroying the only influence which has been effective in modifying the traditional policies of the private power companies—the threat of competition in ideas and results in alternative ways of conducting the power business.

In concluding this discussion, let me try to set the issue of public or private ownership of electric utilities in helpful perspective. To do less would risk serious misunderstanding of the problem under discussion. Moreover, I am well aware of the fact that controversy about public or private ownership occupies the center of the stage in most public discussion of the power question today—as it has for many years.

Strident argument beats with renewed vigor around various projects proposed to develop the rivers of America, the St. Lawrence, the Niagara, the Columbia, and the Snake—with its dramatic power possibilities along Hell's Canyon. Nor is TVA overlooked in such debates.

This issue of public versus private development of power supply is an old one. It is a favorite battleground for the doctrinaires who place profit from ownership above service, who learn too slowly that service, flavored with managerial enterprise, begets profit if the drive for profits is tempered with self-restraint. Against them are arrayed consumer groups who for good reason see water-power sites as a public asset and want to be sure those assets are not wasted by piecemeal small-scale developments which fail to capture that full power of our rivers which only wise and comprehensive development can produce. Nor should governments step aside and let the benefits of these great natural resource developments be diverted from the consumer.

Some of the attacks upon public power spring from a conception of the capitalist system which is distorted and unreal—and sometimes naïve. One would think from some of the speeches one reads that in some undesignated period there existed in this country a utopian classical economy in which the government took no part in economic activities. In the less complex times of past generations the tasks of government in this country were certainly fewer and perhaps simpler than they are today. But from the earliest days of the Republic our governments have participated in economic activities which private agencies either could not do as well or could not or would not do at all. Roads, public docks, the post office, canals, and water-supply systems are only a few examples. One of the great sources of strength of our capitalist system has been the richness and variety of its management resources and devices. In truth TVA and the other public power agencies in this country are not a departure from our capitalist system; they are in fact a valuable part of it. They have introduced the good old device of competition into an otherwise smug cost-plus monopoly industry.

This country's power policy is not going to be determined by impassioned debates over the abstract labels called "socialism," "statism," and "free private enterprise." The final decision as to who provides electric service is going to be decided by the people themselves on a practical basis, case by case. And it will be decided on the basis of how electricity—the lifeblood of a modern economy—may be made available more and more abundantly, through reliable services and at the lowest possible cost to the consumer.

Private corporations generate and sell four-fifths—80 per cent—of all the electric power sold in the United States. The other one-fifth is supplied by public plants and systems owned by the federal and local governments and private consumer–co-operative corporations.

But the electricity business, whoever owns and operates it, is a public business. And it has been so regarded by America for many, many years. This idea is not new, foreign, or alien; it is as native to this land as corn bread. The same can be said for public ownership of electric plants. It has been a part of the American pattern from the beginning of the industry.

Private corporations engaged in the electric business enjoy privileges granted by the public through law, franchise, or license. They use the public streets and roads as rights of way for poles, lines, and underground circuits; they are permitted to exercise the sovereign right of eminent domain to secure land and right of way for their plants and facilities; because of the nature of their function, they are monopolies in the areas they serve; regulatory bodies established by law are commissioned to sanction financial arrangements that assure them a reasonable level of earnings. None of these privileges or prerogatives is granted by the public to electric corporations as a mark of favor. They are granted in order that the companies as a vehicle for prudent investment may perform a public service efficiently.

The operation of an electric system is a managerial job. The managers can be either private or public managers, as the public elects. But, whether managers are hired by a public agency or by a private corporation, the public has a right to expect them to perform a true public function.

If the private utilities satisfy the public objectives of providing low-cost electricity in abundance, they have a good chance of staying in the business. But if they fail the consumers, then the private managers should not be surprised if they are fired by the consumers and replaced by public managers. When private utilities do a good job, as many of them do, there is little public demand for dismissing the private companies as the public's agent. In my view the best way for private power companies to remain private is to show more enterprise.

The question of whether ownership of the utility industry should be in public or private hands has less bearing on the future of the real free enterprise of this country than the quality of utility management. For the quality of management and the policies and practices utility managers pursue, irrespective of ownership, have a lot to do with the growth and greater freedom of American enterprise in thousands of rural communities, towns, and cities. An ample power supply for the nation's growth and security is the primary issue. And the problem today is more pressing than at any time since the beginning of World War II.

A very minimum of prudence suggests that we nourish and hold accountable both private and public ownership in a pattern of vigorous competition in performance, each encouraged to merit public support by its performance of a public service and its contribution to our national strength.

I submit that these are the ingredients and fundamental features of a national power policy that would make sense.

Appendix A. Farms, Fertilizers, and Munitions

Introduction

The origin of the Tennessee Valley Authority's concern with chemical fertilizers dates back to the first World War. At that time the country needed great quantities of nitrogen for munitions to take the place of imported nitrates in danger of being cut off by the war. The production of synthetic nitrogen compounds required cheap electricity. At Muscle Shoals, where the Tennessee River drops swiftly through the slope of northern Alabama, a site had long been identified by engineers as a place to build a great dam useful for power as well as navigation. The nitrate plants were built; Wilson Dam was built. And the acts of Congress which authorized these projects recognized their value to peacetime agriculture as a source of cheaper plant foods which the power of the river and the knowledge of chemists could produce.

Through the 1920's the two nitrate plants stood idle, while the seasonal power generated at Wilson Dam was sold to a private power company. The question of how these structures could best serve agriculture and electricity consumers aroused great interest. Private business groups offered to buy them from the government—at a very large discount. Commissions were appointed by Presidents Coolidge and Hoover to "study and recommend." The subject sharpened into conflict and public debate.

The issue of that day is probably recalled by many as "the Muscle Shoals fight," in which the late George Norris, senator from Nebraska, worked so valiantly and successfully to devote these national wartime assets to a peacetime public purpose. Twice his proposals to establish a TVA were passed by Congress, only to meet with presidential vetoes.

In the South, where the use of fertilizer to gain higher cotton yields was a practice of long standing, the cry for cheaper nitrates dramatized the continued idleness of the Muscle Shoals nitrate plants.

In 1933 Congress established the Tennessee Valley Authority and transferred to it the Muscle Shoals properties then in the custody of the United States Army Corps of Engineers. By the terms of the law the Authority was to maintain these plants for national defense and to use them in peacetime for the manufacture and promotion of new and more efficient fertilizers. It is my purpose in this chapter to discuss these statutory assignments.

During the last twenty years TVA has produced about 2,000,000 tons of phospate products and 1,500,000 tons of nitrates. In addition, large quantities of elemental phosphorus, ammonia, and ammonium nitrates have been furnished to the armed services for munitions. Chemical engineering research applied from test tube through pilot plants and into large-scale production has improved and developed new processes of manufacturing nitrate and phosphorus fertilizers. These developments have influenced the types, amount, and cost of fertilizers produced throughout the country by fertilizer and chemical industries. The products of TVA's chemical plants have been distributed in general on a noncommercial basis for use in demonstration and educational sales programs reaching tens of thousands of individual farmers in the Tennessee Valley and in more than half of the forty-eight states. By these means the Authority has exerted an important and favorable influence upon the use of fertilizer, especially in programs of soil-conserving agriculture.

In 1953 its chemical plants produced about 400,000 tons of fertilizers. This represents less than 3 per cent of the fertilizer used in the United States during that year. It should be recognized, therefore, that TVA's role in this field is not to be measured by the volume of materials it produces but rather by the kinds of processes developed and successfully used and the strategic way the products reach the farmer and his land in some of the important food-production areas of the country.

The function of TVA in relation to fertilizer production, cost, and use is to forge and use a strategic device by which the government assumes the risks of large-scale research and the production of a substantial, though not predominant, volume of new types of materials. The program serves two purposes. One is to develop fertilizer materials which can be economically and effectively used by the farmer to increase production and to build up fertility and conserve the soil. The second is to develop processes and equipment which will enable manufacturers to produce the kind of fertilizers farmers need, at costs they can afford to pay, and at the same time make the best and most economical use of the raw material from which the fertilizers are made.

The Importance of Fertilizer

To the nation's consumers fertilizer assumes its general importance within the framework of increased agricultural production for a constantly increasing population and for an ever rising standard of living. Between 1925 and 1950 the nation's population increased by approximately one-third—from 115,000,000 to 151,000,000—while the output of the nation's farms rose by almost one-half—from $22 billion to $32 billion in terms of 1950 prices.

This rapid expansion of output was achieved without increasing the acres of cropland harvested. Even more remarkable has been the decline in farm employment during this period. In 1925 approximately 13,000,000 workers produced the nation's agricultural output. By 1953 the number of agricultural workers had dropped to less than 10,000,000. But, while the amount of cropland remained unchanged and the amount of labor declined, the use of commercial fertilizer increased by three times (from 1,200,000 tons in 1925 to 4,000,000 tons in 1950).

This is not to suggest that increased use of fertilizer has been the only factor responsible for the remarkable production achievements of our nation's farms over the past quarter-century. Mechanization of the motive power for American agriculture has largely occurred during the last twenty-five years. Development of genetically superior crops, such as hybrid corn and disease-resistant strains of many crops, has been a major factor in increasing farm output. One measure of the importance of fertilizer, however, is found in the fact that American farmers have increased their consumption of commercial fertilizer more than six times as fast as they have increased farm output.

In the Tennessee Valley more efficient fertilizers in greater quantity have played an even more dramatic role. During the last two decades the growth of a livestock agricultural economy in the Southeast has provided a phenomenal contrast with the past. By now this is an old story, and tourists passing through the Tennessee Valley find it a common experience to see green pastures and grazing cattle as well as fields of cotton. Many things contributed to this partial displacement of King Cotton and the row-crop economy. But, until it was learned how to manage the soils of the South for the production of high-quality pasture and forage crops, farmers could not readily make the choice to raise cattle. Fertilizer and lime made possible the introduction of high-quality pasture and hay crops which in turn provided part of the base for an expanding livestock.

Let me illustrate these general statements by an example from an eastern Tennessee farm. Ten years ago this farm was a combination of eroded wasteland and worn-out peach orchards. By careful farm planning, and with a ready market for his product, this farmer borrowed money from the Farm Home Administration and local banks, sought advice from his county agent, learned dairy-management techniques from a field man of the near-by milk plant, and was selected to be a test-demonstration farmer to try out new TVA fertilizers. Now the most-eroded hillside is covered with sturdy pines; corn has been moved to the creek bottoms; and the unproductive wasteland and peach orchard are now fertile pastures. This plan included soil conservation, but the conservation goal was integrated with the other goals of the farm family. The farmer made his plan to embrace improvement of the fertility and productivity of the land; he was not content just to hold the soil where it was in its unproductive state.

On this farm high-analysis fertilizer was needed to make the farmer's conservation plan feasible. Fertilizer introduced a factor of soil-fertility improvement or soil development upon which a well-ordered change in land use could be scheduled over a period of several years or seasons. It is in this "development" sense that fertilizers play an important part in the conservation of agricultural land, a problem in which the Authority has a special responsibility in the Tennessee Valley.

The ABC's of Fertilizer Economics

In order to understand TVA's function in fertilizer experiment and manufacture, it is essential that one know the ABC's of fertilizer economics. The value of fertilizer to the farmer is affected by many factors—how he uses it, on what kinds of soils, when, for what crops, and the markets and prices for which he produces. One factor that makes an immediate difference in the cost of fertilizer to the farmer is the amount of actual plant food contained in the fertilizer material he buys. A 100-pound bag of *low-analysis* fertilizer contains, say, 20 per cent, more or less, of usable plant food. This plant food is usually made up of materials containing nitrogen, phosphorus, and potassium. A part of the other 80 per cent of the bag of fertilizer may or may not be useful.

But, in any case, when the farmer buys a bag of fertilizer, the price includes freight on the full weight of the contents of the bag; the lower the percentage of plant food per bag, the greater his expenses in trucking the material and applying it to the field for each unit of plant food he handles. The land upon which it is spread gets not 100 pounds of plant food but 20 pounds. Now, if a 100-pound bag contained 40 per cent plant food, the cost of bagging at the manufacturing plant, freight, and transportation and labor in using each unit of plant food would be cut in half. And it is important to note that in some—not many, but some—important areas of the country up to 50 per cent of the total cost of a ton of fertilizer delivered to the farmer is transportation cost.

These elementary facts form the basis for much of what TVA has been doing at Muscle Shoals in the last twenty years.

Between 1910 and 1935, the year when farmers in the Tennessee Valley began to receive TVA's concentrated superphosphate from the rebuilt Muscle Shoals chemical facilities, the average amount of plant food contained in all commercial mixed fertilizers used in the United States rose slowly from 14 per cent in 1910 to about 18 per cent in 1935. (By 1952 the average plant-food content of all mixed fertilizers used in the United States had risen to about 25 per cent.) The average phosphate content of all commercial fertilizers rose even less—almost not at all—in *the same period* (from 9.0 per cent in 1910 to only 9.14 per cent in 1935).

This painfully slow trend toward higher-analysis, more efficient fertilizer materials was not primarily due to a lack of technical knowledge. Concentrated superphosphate was first produced in the United States in 1890. By 1935, however, production of concentrated superphosphate (private manufacturers and TVA) amounted to little more than 90,000 tons and provided less than 8 per cent of the available plant nutrients provided by phosphate fertilizers. Progress had been so slow that in 1933, when Congress was considering the creation of TVA, the president of the American Farm Bureau Federation stated before a congressional committee that the production and distribution methods of the fertilizer industry were "as antiquated as the ox cart would be passing down Pennsylvania Avenue."[1]

Numerous reasons have been advanced to explain why the fertilizer industry was slow to adopt more efficient methods of production and marketing. Some investigations have pointed to the early adoption by American farmers of the mixed fertilizers developed as a country-cousin outlet for the wastes or by-products of manufacturers who were primarily interested in other things. Once farmers became accustomed to mixed fertilizers, the inertia of buying habits, reluctance among farmers to try new products, and the vested position of the small

1. *Muscle Shoals* (House Report 48 [73d Cong., 1st sess. (Washington, D.C., 1933)]), p. 83.

mixer plants combined to discourage aggressive marketing policies. Others have contended that the restraining hand of monopolistic collusion among domestic producers of raw materials and the existence of an international cartel in the phosphate rock industry were the major factors holding back technical innovation in the industry. It is not important at this time to take sides, because the last twenty years have witnessed the beginning of a favorable change.

By 1933 the demands of American farmers for cheaper and more efficient fertilizers could no longer be held back. When the TVA Act was passed, the new agency was given authority to attack the fertilizer problem on several fronts. The Act specified that the Authority was to use its resources to advance and improve fertilizer technology; to manufacture fertilizer; and to arrange with farmers and farm organizations to demonstrate in large-scale, practical ways the economic value of new forms of fertilizers.

TVA's Decision To Produce High-Analysis Phosphate Fertilizer

Nitrogen and phosphate products were mentioned specifically in the Act, but the board decided to emphasize high-analysis phosphate fertilizers rather than nitrogen or potash. This decision was based upon careful consideration of the needs of agriculture, the technology of fertilizer manufacture, the opportunity to relate phosphate deposits more efficiently to areas of fertilizer need and conserve phosphate reserves, and the best ways to contribute to the national defense.

In 1933 phosphate was regarded by agricultural scientists familiar with the Tennessee Valley region as the principal limiting factor in the soils of the Valley and the South. Experts from the state colleges and the United States Department of Agriculture advised the board that nitrates were readily available to farmers if they grew legumes which could capture this element from the air and through their root systems put it into the soil. But legumes would not grow readily in a soil without phosphate, and soil minerals, especially phosphate, were present in only limited quantities in many soils of the nation. Because of this farmers living on mineral-deficient soils were hindered in growing the kinds of plants and in developing the kinds of farm systems which would conserve soil and water, produce nutritious food and feed, and give them the greater economic flexibility inherent in diversified farming.

A joint congressional committee in 1939 reported that "soil scientists told this committee that four-fifths of the soils of America are now deficient in phosphorus. Each year they estimate that several million tons of this vital element are being lost through erosion and cropping. Permitted to continue, this loss of phosphorus will proceed at an accelerated rate."[2]

In the Tennessee Valley itself it has been all too apparent for years that something was wrong with agriculture. Erosion, abandoned and wasted land, scrub pine, poverty grass, and broom sedge—the symptoms of a mineral-poor land—were all too common. Phosphate with lime and some potash, properly used, held the hope of making it possible to substitute legumes and improved pastures and meadows for erosive corn and cotton row crops.

Chemical fertilizer is an old story to the farmer of the South. By 1933, although the South used the bulk of fertilizers consumed in the country, the soil and the agriculture of the Tennessee Valley and the South remained poor and were getting poorer all the time. This fact was grim testimony that fertilizer alone, fertilizer not accompanied by far-reaching changes in the use of land, did not build up and maintain soil fertility. The experts knew this. The late Harcourt A. Morgan, a member of the original TVA board, with a long record of experience as an agricultural scientist, knew this. Many farmers knew it too. But phosphate fertilizers were expensive when purchased in low-analysis mixtures, and the changes in cropping practices advocated by the experts involved substantial risk to the farmer.

Technologically, opportunities appeared greatest with phosphates. Industrial processes for nitrogen production had advanced so rapidly since 1918 that research possibilities did not appear particularly chal-

2. *Phosphate Resources of the United States* (Senate Doc. 21 [76th Cong., 1st sess. (Washington, D.C., 1939)]), p. 2.

lenging in that field. In fact, the rapid advance of knowledge had outmoded, almost by the time they were built, the two nitrate plants TVA inherited from World War I. The mining and refining of potash involve a rather simple technology and seemed to offer little chance for technological development. In contrast, phosphate appeared to present an opportunity for important advance. The combination of available phosphate-ore deposits in Tennessee, low-cost electric power resulting from the development of the Tennessee River, and the high transportation costs involved in the distribution of low-analysis fertilizers made experimentation in the production of high-analysis phosphate fertilizers with electric-furnace methods especially attractive.

The decision to develop high-analysis phosphate fertilizers was especially important in terms of long-run conservation and use of the nation's phosphate reserves. The known economically minable reserve of phosphate rock in the United States is estimated at a few billion tons; in addition, perhaps double or treble that amount is in somewhat lower-grade rock not considered economically minable without the development of new processing methods. Two facts underscore the importance of using our phosphate reserves wisely: it is an exhaustible resource for which there is no substitute and the need for phosphates on the land is very great.

These reserves are centered principally in three areas. Middle Tennessee accounts for, say, less than 1 per cent, and Florida about one-third of the total. The largest reserves are located in the four western states of Idaho, Utah, Montana, and Wyoming. In 1933 almost none of the nation's phosphate production was using these great western reserves. There were and are many reasons for this. But one very important reason is the distance from the western phosphate deposits to the great potential market in the nation's breadbasket, the upper Mississippi Valley.

The opening of the western phosphate reserves for use in the Midwest depends in large part on reduction of transportation cost. This can be achieved through the development and adoption of low-cost methods of producing high-analysis phosphate fertilizers. A 20 per cent phosphate fertilizer produced from western reserves would cost too much on an Illinois farm. But a 62 per cent phosphate fertilizer, such as TVA has since developed, might enable manufacturers to ship western phosphates to the Midwest at economically feasible costs. This would also relieve the excessive drain on the small deposits in Tennessee. Moreover, new processes offer the prospect of using lower-grade phosphate ores. Thus the Authority through chemical research, might furnish a foundation for a wise conservation policy which would encourage prudent use of our phosphate reserves and more efficient management of the soil.

In deciding to pioneer in phosphate research and development, the board in 1933 saw an opportunity to enhance the national defense value of the Muscle Shoals installations. While nitrate plant No. 1 was held in stand-by condition, nitrate plant No. 2 was to be rebuilt with electric furnaces to produce elemental phosphorus. This product could be processed to make fertilizer one day and munitions the next. The close technical bond between fertilizer and munitions supported the idea of using the same laboratories, plants, and technicians for work on both.

Contributions of TVA's Fertilizer Program

Beginning in the summer of 1933, under the direction of Dr. Harry A. Curtis, TVA's first chief chemical engineer (presently a member of the board of directors), a staff of chemists and chemical engineers was assembled, an operating force recruited and trained, and the task of rehabilitating the old plant was begun. Dr. Curtis had been associated with various phases of the design and reappraisal of these nitrate plants during and after World War I and was intimately familiar with the difficulties inherent in their use.

The first of the Authority's fertilizer production units went into operation at Muscle Shoals in late 1934. In 1935, the first full year of operation, it produced about 24,000 tons of concentrated superphosphate. In 1953 the Authority produced 136,000 tons of this material, 42,000 tons of calcium metaphosphate, 26,000 tons of fused tricalcium phosphare, and 197,000 tons of ammonium nitrate. These products are processed in a large-scale plant operation. In pilot plants smaller quantities of nitric phosphates, diammonium phosphates, and other experimental materials are also produced.

The value of any research program depends upon a wise choice of projects for study. The world situation governs the extent to which TVA uses personnel and facilities on munitions projects. Even at the height of World War II, however, fertilizer was so essential to the food supply of the Great Alliance that the Authority continued work on important fertilizer projects while producing large quantities of munitions. When ships were carrying cargoes to England, phosphate fertilizer for England's food-crop program was an important item. TVA's new and experimental product, 62 per cent P_2O_5—calcium metaphosphate—took much less cargo space than a 20 or 40 per cent material.

Most of the board's fertilizer research and large-plant experiments try to find a way to lower the cost of fertilizer by developing a process to produce new fertilizers or by improving processes already in use. When an idea for a new process is found, it is first evaluated for its technical and economic possibilities, taking full advantage of fundamental research and the published information. When a process looks good enough for experimental study, the various steps are tested in small-scale laboratory equipment. These tests provide information about the conditions required to produce the new material. They also yield enough of the material for tests in greenhouse and field trials at the state agricultural experiment stations. If the process and the product look promising, a pilot plant is built to furnish data for cost estimates and for the design of a large-scale plant.

Successful operation of a pilot plant alone is not always enough to encourage industry to adopt the process. In fact, the process cannot be judged fully until it has stood the test of large-scale operations. Costs must be favorable, and the new product must have proved itself in the market. If the product differs from ordinary fertilizers, farmers may hesitate to use it even when it offers advantages to them. Operation of the plant produces enough of the fertilizer for testing on a large scale by thousands of farmers on their farms. If it works well in farm operations, farmer acceptance may convince commercial producers that a market for the new product is assured. By thus reducing the risk which impedes development of new processes and production by industry, TVA helps to speed up improvements in the technology of fertilizer manufacture.

Between 1934 and 1953, through its chemical and engineering staff and facilities at Muscle Shoals, the board has undertaken research and development work on some fifteen or twenty fertilizer materials. But present activity is centered around four fertilizers which are in advanced stages of development, plus a number of relatively new multiple-nutrient fertilizers. The products which are now in advanced stages of development are concentrated superphosphate (48 per cent P_2O_5); ammonium nitrate fertilizer (33.5 per cent N); calcium metaphosphate (62 per cent P_2O_5); and fused tricalcium phosphate (28 per cent P_2O_5—ordinary superphosphate on the market is about 18 or 22 per cent). These materials, along with urea (45–46 per cent N) and anhydrous ammonia (82 per cent N), are now rapidly replacing ordinary superphosphate, nitrate of soda (16 per cent N), and ammonium sulphate (20.5 per cent N) for use on most crops. All these older products are low-analysis materials and therefore more expensive for most farmers.

The Phosphate Story

From the beginning, this fertilizer research and development program has been, in large part, a phosphate story. Since 1934, TVA has produced and distributed 1,500,000 tons of *concentrated superphosphate*, or about 24 per cent of the total national production of this material for that period. In the latest fiscal year, 1953, the Authority's production of concentrated superphosphate was only about 15 per cent of the national output.

Today, concentrated superphosphate is firmly established as a commercial product. But, when TVA began national production, the material was very limited. The promotion of this product has had something to do with the accelerated trend toward higher-analysis phosphate materials. While the average phosphate content of all commercial fertilizers showed almost no increase in the twenty-five years preceding TVA, average phosphate content has risen from 9 per cent in 1935 to 12 per cent in 1952. I am not suggesting that the Authority can take all the credit for this favorable trend; it is safe to assert, however, that its work had a great deal to do with it. By 1952 private production of concentrated superphosphate had increased about eleven times (from 66,727 tons in 1935 to 727,059 tons in 1952). It is estimated that the 1952 level of national output will double by 1955. At the present time this high-analysis product supplies about 25 per cent of the phosphate plant food used as fertilizer. Private manufacturers have picked it up as a good product. Consequently, TVA will soon withdraw from the production of concentrated superphosphate.

Work on *calcium metaphosphate*—a new fertilizer that has been developed in the Muscle Shoals laboratories—began in 1935 and had passed through the pilot-plant stage to production scale by 1938. Only in the last year, however, has the process finally been brought to a relatively satisfactory technical position. Because of its very high analysis and the large amounts of power required to produce it, this material has advantages over other fertilizers for production in the West, where power costs can be low. (The full development of the Hell's Canyon power projects in Idaho has a bearing on this.) This process and product can reduce the high cost of transportation to the major fertilizer markets in the Middle West. The same freight cost on a bag of this material will carry three times as many units of plant food as ordinary superphosphate and about one and a third as many units as concentrated superphosphate.

Private industry is now considering the construction of several production units in the West. One of the farm co-operative federations with long experience in the distribution and use of TVA materials has acquired phosphate-ore reserves in the West and hopes to build a processing plant. In the meantime this co-operative is buying calcium metaphosphate from the Authority and using it in the production of a high-analysis mixed fertilizer. This arrangement would establish a market and lay a basis for the co-operative to build a western plant and substitute its own calcium metaphosphate for an interim supply. This type of arrangement to use the Authority as an interim source of supply to obtain expansion and modernization of fertilizer production holds great promise. The board plans to continue the production of calcium metaphosphate until a few industry groups actually begin producing it in considerable quantities. When that happens, TVA will push another process and product, of higher concentration, into trial and use.

Fused tricalcium phosphate, like calcium metaphosphate, has required a long period of experimental and developmental work. Research on the process has been carried on by the board intermittently from 1933 to the present, but it has not yet been adopted for commercial production. The major technical engineering problems have been solved, and the agronomic value of the product has been fairly well established.

This process has a number of advantages over conventional methods used to manufacture phosphate fertilizers—it requires no sulfur or sulfuric acid and uses phosphate ore of lower grade than is suitable for ordinary processes. The product is especially effective on grass and legume forage crops because it releases its plant-food content over a longer period of time than other fertilizers. The material itself seems well suited to bulk distribution and storage, as few other fertilizers are. On the other hand, the product is well adapted only to certain parts of the country. It is not, for example, effective upon the alkaline soils of the West. It cannot be mixed chemically with some other fertilizer ingredients. TVA has carried this project as far as it can go for the present and plans shortly to discontinue it. This material is not likely to be adopted for commercial production until special circumstances affecting markets and raw materials match its special advantages.

The Ammonium Nitrate Story

While TVA was developing electric-furnace processes for new phosphate fertilizers, it kept the obsolete ammonium nitrate plant from World War I in stand-by condition to produce munitions if the need arose. In 1942 the Chemical Corps of the United States Army asked the board to produce ammonium nitrate for munitions. This could have been done by tinkering with the old World War I plant—a costly prospect. The old graining facilities were too dangerous to use, and new ones were built. A new ammonia plant to supply the graining facilities would save money. The Authority, therefore, built a modern ammonia plant with funds provided at the request of the War Department and the President.[3] During the war TVA supplied 64,000 tons of ammonium nitrate explosives for military purposes.

In the meantime, as the agricultural needs for nitrogen were increasing, it was apparent that ammonium nitrate could become an important and cheaper nitrogen fertilizer. Ammonium nitrate has a higher nitrogen content than any other solid fertilizer material except urea. TVA, the United States Department of Agriculture, and industrial concerns, therefore, began to devise ways to condition this munitions material for agricultural use.

The ammonium nitrate phase of production (as distinguished from ammonia production) involved hazardous operations, and plans were developed to revise and modernize the old plant. The new capacity developed by the Authority, along with new capacity financed by the government and leased or sold to private companies since the war, has helped to meet the rapidly expanding demand of the nation for nitrogen fertilizer. A large share of TVA's output has been distributed through contracts with farm co-operatives and private dealers at prices in the lower market range to reflect the low costs of production. (And

3. For an interesting and illuminating example of an "industry versus government" argument about anticipated postwar control of ammonia plant production capacity see Committee on Public Administration Cases, *The TVA Ammonia Plant* (Washington, D.C.: The Committee, 1950). Also in Harold Stein (ed.), *Public Administration and Policy Development* (New York: Harcourt, Brace & Co., 1952), pp. 391–444.

these low prices are feasible in spite of the fact that this ammonia plant is the only one among the plants built by the government during World War II that is being amortized at its full wartime cost.) A portion of TVA's ammonium nitrate was made available at special discounts to promote new and special uses of ammonium nitrate fertilizer to fit the requirements of soil-conserving farm plans.

Today, ammonium nitrate is well on the way to becoming the major nitrogen fertilizer in this country. Production of this material, first manufactured for sale as a fertilizer in the United States in 1943, grew to an estimated 634,000 tons in 1951. By 1956 solid ammonium nitrate capacity is expected to reach approximately 1,375,000 tons. Again, as in the case of concentrated superphosphate, the board plans to shift its ammonia supplies to the production of new fertilizers, as production of ammonium nitrate by private industry increases.

In addition to these products of major attention over the last fifteen years, several promising new, extremely high-analysis, multiple-nutrient carriers of phosphorus and nitrogen, and also phosphorus, nitrogen, and potassium, are now being developed in the laboratories and pilot plants. Some of these developments are appropriate for commercial adoption from pilot-plant experience alone without undue risk. An example is the acidulation of rock phosphate with mixtures of sulfuric and phosphoric acids. This is a co-operative project arranged between TVA and the United States Department of Agriculture in connection with the Atomic Energy Commission. The AEC contemplates the production by industry of large quantities of phosphoric acid by the wet process, that is, using sulphuric acid on phosphate rock. The sulfuric acid to be used for this purpose will be diverted from the manufacture of ordinary superphosphate, and the phosphoric acid that is produced, after being treated for recovery of uranium, will be turned over to superphosphate manufacturers for use in their plants. Technical information will be required to assist the small manufacturers of ordinary low-concentrate superphosphate if they are to succeed in this program.

Another process which is being followed with considerable interest at the present time is TVA's pilot-plant work on nitric phosphate processes, in which nitric acid is substituted for sulfuric acid in treating phosphate material. This process offers the industry an opportunity to expand production of nitrogen materials and thereby reduce costs. The nitric phosphate products also can be used to produce, economically, higher-analysis fertilizers.

One of these nitric phosphate processes, developed through the pilot-plant stage, will soon be put into commercial production by Associated Co-operatives, a large federation of farm co-operatives reaching the South and Far West. A large private producer of nitrogen products built a nitric phosphate plant and started production a few months ago.

TVA is working on other multiple-nutrient products, so named because they are chemical mixtures capable of carrying a higher plant-food content than physical mixtures of materials containing the basic chemicals. Two of these now being carried through the laboratory and pilot-plant stages are diammonium phosphate, which contains approximately 70 per cent plant food (20 per cent N, 50 per cent P_2O_5), and ammonium metaphosphate (17–20 per cent N, 73–80 per cent P_2O_5), a material of very high concentration.

Technical Assistance to Industry

The chemists and engineers engaged in fertilizer research and development at Muscle Shoals have come upon many patentable processes, mechanical devices, and pieces of equipment. To date, more than a hundred United States patents have been issued to employees and assigned to TVA. While these patents are secured primarily to safeguard use of inventions made by its employees, TVA grants royalty-free, nonexclusive licenses to industrial concerns for their use.

A number of private firms have found it advantageous to arrange for such licenses. For example, one of the patents covers a continuous mixing process developed for the manufacture of concentrated superphosphate. This has been licensed both to producing companies that wish to use the process in their own operations and to engineering firms that design and construct equipment for manufacturers.

TVA welcomes such use of its inventions by industry as a means of promoting improved and more efficient fertilizer manufacture. Its plants are always open for inspection and study by industry representatives. Last year alone, seven hundred visitors came to the Muscle Shoals chemical plants to study the work, and more than nine hundred requests for technical information were answered by mail. Three chemical engineering reports were issued, making a total of nine such reports so far published dealing with major research projects carried on at Muscle Shoals. In addition, about 160 papers describing these fertilizer research and development activities have appeared in technical journals. The National Fertilizer Association cooperates with TVA in bringing the results of its research to the attention of private industry.

During the past year several large firms, all of which have been assisted by TVA's research, designs, and information, put new electric furnaces into operation. Western phosphate reserves were developed further by the expansion of electric-furnace facilities in that part of the country. The Monsanto Chemical Company started operation of a new and very large furnace in Idaho. The Westvaco Chemical Division of the Food Machinery and Chemical Corporation put its fourth furnace into operation, and the Victor Chemical Company started its second western furnace in Montana. In Tennessee the Shea Chemical Company began production of dicalcium phosphate. The phosphorus electric furnace used by the Shea concern in the process is based on TVA's designs; the company is licensed to use four TVA patents for making elemental phosphorus and another for expanding electric-furnace slag to make light-weight building material. In Florida the American Agricultural Chemical Company obtained very satisfactory results in operation of its new rotating-type furnace, the design of which was based on the Authority's pioneer development.

Demonstrations and Distribution of TVA's Fertilizers

Technical processes are, of course, only one part of the fertilizer program. The Act authorized arrangements with farmers and farm organizations for large-scale, practical use of the new forms of fertilizers to be developed at Muscle Shoals. It also authorized co-operation with experiment stations, farmers, and others in an effort to prevent soil erosion by the use of fertilizers. In carrying out this assignment, the board has developed working arrangements with many groups, including co-operatives and a number of fertilizer-manufacturing companies.

The output of a full-scale demonstration plant provides enough material for carrying on a program to introduce the product on practical farms in normal farm operation. This is accomplished, primarily, through the farm test-demonstration program, now operating in twenty-five states. This program is administered in the states by the agricultural extension services and sponsored in the counties by farmer organizations which, with advice from county agents, select the test-demonstration farms and distribute TVA's fertilizer. Test-demonstration farms are selected to represent, in so far as possible, a cross-section of agricultural conditions, including soil types, size of farms, and types of farming. In this way farmers in widely scattered areas obtain quantities of the new product, use it as recommended by the agricultural colleges, and learn for themselves and demonstrate to their neighbors what it will contribute to their operation.

Significantly, in following the recommended changes in their farm planning, most of the farmers must supplement the test-demonstration fertilizer they receive with other materials from commercial sources. In the fifteen-year period ending in 1949 the use of commercial fertilizer in the Tennessee Valley, where the test demonstrations are concentrated, increased three times as fast as in the rest of the nation.

TVA's fertilizer products in excess of those needed in these intensive tests and demonstrations are sold through selected farmer co-operatives and commercial distributors for specified new and improved uses by farmers. One of the objectives of this sales program is to use the products of TVA in a manner which will result in better farming practices and an expanded market for high-analysis fertilizers. The particular uses to be made of these fertilizers are agreed upon in meetings with the land-grant colleges, agencies of the USDA, and distributors. The uses vary from state to state, depending on the practices which, in the opinion of the co-operating groups and agencies, will contribute most to better and more productive land use.

In these sales of TVA's fertilizers through selected market channels, the final responsibility for getting the materials into the uses that have been approved rests with the distributors. The distribution contract provides that the amount of fertilizer received by any distributor will be directly related to his performance in carrying out the program of new and better uses.

Contributions to National Defense

In addition to its contributions to agriculture and the advancement of fertilizer technology, the national defense value of the Muscle Shoals facilities has been restored and expanded. Both nitrogen and phosphorus have double roles : they are plant foods and key ingredients for munitions. With the outbreak of World War II, the facilities of TVA were quickly mobilized for munitions research and development.

During World War II the board supplied more than 60 per cent of the elemental phosphorus required by our armed forces for use in smoke and incendiary bombs, shells, tracer bullets, and other munitions. During the war TVA also delivered some 30,000 tons of anhydrous ammonia, 10,000 tons of ammonium nitrate liquor, and 64,000 tons of ammonium nitrate crystal to the United States Ordnance Department. It also produced more than 200,000 tons of calcium carbide for the manufacture of synthetic rubber, using rehabilitated equipment which had been in stand-by condition since World War I.

At this stage in our history there can be little question that the Muscle Shoals chemical plants and the Authority's staff of chemists and chemical engineers are an important asset for the national defense.

They likewise will continue to have an important place in the future of American agriculture, peace or war. With mounting crop surpluses and sliding farm prices, this statement may require explanation. Plans to continue fertilizer development and production rest on two basic assumptions: our population will continue to grow and our standard of living will continue to rise.

In spite of current agricultural surpluses, most forecasters predict a rather rapid growth in the demand for farm products during the next twenty-five years. Present population estimates indicate a 1975 population of between 199,000,000 and 221,000,000. The combination of increased population and rising per capita income could easily result in a 60 per cent increase in the demand for farm products between 1950 and 1975. And one should not forget the multiplying peoples elsewhere in the world, whose aspirations for a higher standard of living are not beyond the range of our enlightened self-interest.

To meet this greatly increased demand, the United States is fortunate in having enviable facilities for agricultural production. We have many lands superbly adapted to machine agriculture, and production per acre has steadily increased throughout our history. But land can show the ravages of age as its use increases. The mineral nutrients in the soil can be used up. Since the future extent of our cultivated land is expected to remain about the same, this in itself means more fertilizer, even to produce the same output as now. A still larger production means more productive crops, and they in turn may mean greater demands for fertilizer.

As far as the near future is concerned, an adequate supply of fertilizers seems assured. If current plant expansion and construction plans are realized, fertilizer production will reach the level required to meet 1959–60 requirements by 1956 or 1957. The long-run (1950–75) picture is somewhat less certain. The Paley Commission has estimated that total fertilizer consumption in 1975 should be approximately 150 per cent above the 1950 level.[4] More recent farm-output re-

4. "United States Fertilizer Resources," in President's Materials Policy Commission, *Resources for Freedom* (Washington, D.C.: Government Printing Office, 1952), V, 76–82.

quirement estimates, based on revised population projections, indicate that fertilizer requirements may be 225 per cent above the 1950 level by 1975.

The accuracy of these long-run estimates is difficult to judge. They are enough, however, to tell us that an abundant fertilizer supply will not be achieved without planning and technical progress. They are enough to tell us that fertilizers at low cost to the farmer will be more important than ever, for, as dependence must be more on commercial fertilizer and less on natural fertility, fertilizer cost is increasingly important. Laboratory research, new processes, new products, better distribution—these are essential if costs are to be reduced.

The job of the chemical engineer and the experimental plant in cost reduction is further emphasized by changes in the character of raw-material sources for phosphate fertilizers. As fertilizer and other demands for phosphorus increase, the United States is having to turn to lower-grade rock and to deposits distant from our major fertilizer-consuming areas. To offset these changes, we must develop still lower cost production and distribution. We need still more efficient use of fertilizers on the farm. TVA, in co-operation with college experiment stations and extension staffs, can help to redress the balance again, as it has in these last twenty years.

How well and quickly the objectives to which TVA is committed are achieved depends in large part upon the farmer and the fertilizer industry. If industry takes over a new process and supplies the demand for the new material—demand developed by the Authority—facilities can be devoted to another promising process or product. Thus the success of this program depends heavily on the extent to which fertilizer manufacturers and distributors follow through beyond the points of research and demonstration where TVA stops.

Finally, we must also take care to preserve a balance among our essential technical services. The science of soils and the study of techniques of fertilization only now are commencing to open the great field which lies before them. As we learn more about plant physiology and nutrition, soil chemistry and physics, and the composition of the thousands of individual soils, new demands are certain to be placed on the fertilizer-production technologist from these sources. Laboratories and facilities for experimental production like those at Muscle Shoals will be needed more than ever before.

Within this setting of an expanding population and growing requirements for food and fibers, limited land resources, and a declining agricultural employment, a program for cheaper fertilizers and improved use of fertilizers thus will continue to be of great significance. The authors of the National Defense Act of 1916 and the framers of the Tennessee Valley Authority Act of 1933, who made Muscle Shoals a center of national significance, contributed more than they may have realized.

Appendix B. Tennessee Valley Authority Act

[PUBLIC—NO. 17—73D CONGRESS, 1ST SESSION]
[H.R. 5081]
May 18, 1933, 48 Stat. 58

[As amended by Public—No. 412—74th Congress, 1st Session]
[H.R. 8632]
August 31, 1935, 49 Stat. 1075

[As amended by Public—No. 224—76th Congress, 1st Session]
[S. 1796]
July 26, 1939, 53 Stat. 1083

[As amended by Public Resolution—No. 88—76th Congress, 3d Session]
[H.J. Res. 544]
June 26, 1940, 54 Stat. 611

[As amended by Public—No. 184—77th Congress, 1st Session]
[H.R. 2097]
July 18, 1941, 55 Stat. 599

[As amended by Public—No. 306—77th Congress, 1st Session]
[H.R. 4961]
November 21, 1941, 55 Stat. 775

AN ACT

To improve the navigability and to provide for the flood control of the Tennessee River; to provide for reforestation and the proper use of marginal lands in the Tennessee Valley; to provide for the agricultural and industrial development of said valley; to provide for the national defense by the creation of a corporation for the operation of Government properties at and near Muscle Shoals in the State of Alabama, and for other purposes

Be it enacted by the Senate and House of Representatives of the United States of America in Congress assembled, That for the purpose of maintaining and operating the properties now owned by the United States in the vicinity of Muscle Shoals, Alabama, in the interest of the national defense and for agricultural and industrial development, and to improve navigation in the Tennessee River and to control the destructive flood waters in the Tennessee River and Mississippi River Basins, there is hereby created a body corporate by the name of the "Tennessee Valley Authority" (hereinafter referred to as the "Corporation"). The board of directors first appointed shall be deemed the incorporators, and the incorporation shall be held to have been effected from the date of the first meeting of the board. This Act may be cited as the "Tennessee Valley Authority Act of 1933." [48 Stat. 58–59.]*

SEC. 2. (a) The board of directors of the Corporation (hereinafter referred to as the "board") shall be composed of three members, to be appointed by the President, by and with the advice and consent of the Senate. In appointing the members of the board, the President shall designate the chairman. All other officials, agents, and employees shall be designated and selected by the board.

(b) The terms of office of the members first taking office after the approval of this Act shall expire as designated by the President at the time of nomination, one at the end of the third year, one at the end of the sixth year, and one at the end of the ninth year, after the date of approval of this Act. A successor to a member of the board shall be appointed in the same manner as the original members and shall have a term of office expiring nine years from the date of the expiration of the term for which his predecessor was appointed.

(c) Any member appointed to fill a vacancy in the board occurring prior to the expiration of the term for which his predecessor was appointed shall be appointed for the remainder of such term.

(d) Vacancies in the board so long as there shall be two members in office shall not impair the powers of the board to execute the functions of the Corporation, and two of the members in office shall constitute a quorum for the transaction of the business of the board.

(e) Each of the members of the board shall be a citizen of the United States, and shall receive a salary at the rate of $10,000† a year, to be paid by the Corporation as current expenses. Each member of the board, in addition to his salary, shall be permitted to occupy as his residence one of the dwelling houses owned by the Government in the vicinity of Muscle Shoals, Alabama, the same to be designated by the President of the United States. Members of the board shall be reimbursed by the Corporation for actual expenses (includ-

* For the purpose of identifying the sections which appeared in the original act of 1933 and those which have been brought into the act by amendment, references have been placed at the end of the sections. For example, the reference at the end of section 1, 48 Stat. 58–59, indicates that this section will be found in volume 48 of the Statutes at Large on pages 58 to 59. All sections will be found in volumes 48, 49, 53, 54, and 55 of the Statutes at Large as indicated.

† Increased to $15,000 a year by 63 Stat. 880.

ing traveling and subsistence expenses) incurred by them in the performance of the duties vested in the board by this Act. No member of said board shall, during his continuance in office, be engaged in any other business, but each member shall devote himself to the work of the Corporation.

(f) No director shall have financial interest in any public-utility corporation engaged in the business of distributing and selling power to the public nor in any corporation engaged in the manufacture, selling, or distribution of fixed nitrogen or fertilizer, or any ingredients thereof, nor shall any member have any interest in any business that may be adversely affected by the success of the Corporation as a producer of concentrated fertilizers or as a producer of electric power.

(g) The board shall direct the exercise of all the powers of the Corporation.

(h) All members of the board shall be persons who profess a belief in the feasibility and wisdom of this Act. [48 Stat. 59.]

Sec. 3. The board shall without regard to the provisions of Civil Service laws applicable to officers and employees of the United States, appoint such managers, assistant managers, officers, employees, attorneys, and agents, as are necessary for the transaction of its business, fix their compensation, define their duties, require bonds of such of them as the board may designate, and provide a system of organization to fix responsibility and promote efficiency. Any appointee of the board may be removed in the discretion of the board. No regular officer or employee of the Corporation shall receive a salary in excess of that received by the members of the board.

All contracts to which the Corporation is a party and which require the employment of laborers and mechanics in the construction, alteration, maintenance, or repair of buildings, dams, locks, or other projects shall contain a provision that not less than the prevailing rate of wages for work of a similar nature prevailing in the vicinity shall be paid to such laborers or mechanics.

In the event any dispute arises as to what are the prevailing rates of wages, the question shall be referred to the Secretary of Labor for determination, and his decision shall be final. In the determination of such prevailing rate or rates, due regard shall be given to those rates which have been secured through collective agreement by representatives of employers and employees.

Where such work as is described in the two preceding paragraphs is done directly by the Corporation the prevailing rate of wages shall be paid in the same manner as though such work had been let by contract.

Insofar as applicable, the benefits of the Act entitled "An Act to provide compensation for employees of the United States suffering injuries while in the performance of their duties, and for other purposes," approved September

7, 1916, as amended, shall extend to persons given employment under the provisions of this Act. [48 Stat. 59–60.]

SEC. 4. Except as otherwise specifically provided in this Act, the Corporation—

(a) Shall have succession in its corporate name.

(b) May sue and be sued in its corporate name.

(c) May adopt and use a corporate seal, which shall be judicially noticed.

(d) May make contracts, as herein authorized.

(e) May adopt, amend, and repeal bylaws.

(f) May purchase or lease and hold such real and personal property as it deems necessary or convenient in the transaction of its business, and may dispose of any such personal property held by it.

The board shall select a treasurer and as many assistant treasurers as it deems proper, which treasurer and assistant treasurers shall give such bonds for the safe-keeping of the securities and moneys of the said Corporation as the board may require: *Provided*, That any member of said board may be removed from office at any time by a concurrent resolution of the Senate and the House of Representatives.

(g) Shall have such powers as may be necessary or appropriate for the exercise of the powers herein specifically conferred upon the Corporation.

(h) Shall have power in the name of the United States of America to exercise the right of eminent domain, and in the purchase of any real estate or the acquisition of real estate by condemnation proceedings, the title to such real estate shall be taken in the name of the United States of America, and thereupon all such real estate shall be entrusted to the Corporation as the agent of the United States to accomplish the purposes of this Act.

(i) Shall have power to acquire real estate for the construction of dams, reservoirs, transmission lines, power houses, and other structures, and navigation projects at any point along the Tennessee River, or any of its tributaries, and in the event that the owner or owners of such property shall fail and refuse to sell to the Corporation at a price deemed fair and reasonable by the board, then the Corporation may proceed to exercise the right of eminent domain, and to condemn all property that it deems necessary for carrying out the purposes of this Act, and all such condemnation proceedings shall be had pursuant to the provisions and requirements hereinafter specified, with reference to any and all condemnation proceedings [48 Stat. 60–61]: *Provided*, That nothing contained herein or elsewhere in this Act shall be construed to deprive the Corporation of the rights conferred by the Act of February 26, 1931 (46 Stat. 1422, ch. 307, secs. 1 to 5, inclusive), as now compiled in section 258a to 258e, inclusive, of Title 40 of the United States Code. [49 Stat. 1075.]

(j) Shall have power to construct such dams, and reservoirs, in the Tennessee River and its tributaries, as in conjunction with Wilson Dam, and Norris, Wheeler, and Pickwick Landing Dams, now under construction, will provide a nine-foot channel in the said river and maintain a water supply for the same, from Knoxville to its mouth, and will best serve to promote navigation on the Tennessee River and its tributaries and control destructive flood waters in the Tennessee and Mississippi River drainage basins; and shall have power to acquire or construct power houses, power structures, transmission lines, navigation projects, and incidental works in the Tennessee River and its tributaries, and to unite the various power installations into one or more systems by transmission lines. The directors of the Authority are hereby directed to report to Congress their recommendations not later than April 1, 1936, for the unified development of the Tennessee River system. [48 Stat. 61, as amended by 49 Stat. 1075.]

(k) Shall have power in the name of the United States—

(*a*) to convey by deed, lease, or otherwise, any real property in the possession of or under the control of the Corporation to any person or persons, for the purpose of recreation or use as a summer residence, or for the operation on such premises of pleasure resorts for boating, fishing, bathing, or any similar purpose;

(*b*) to convey by deed, lease, or otherwise, the possession and control of any such real property to any corporation, partnership, person, or persons for the purpose of erecting thereon docks and buildings for shipping purposes or the manufacture or storage thereon of products for the purpose of trading or shipping in transportation: *Provided*, That no transfer authorized herein in (b) shall be made without the approval of Congress: *And provided further*, That said Corporation, without further action of Congress, shall have power to convey by deed, lease, or otherwise, to the Ingalls Shipbuilding Corporation, a tract or tracts of land at or near Decatur, Alabama, and to the Commercial Barge Lines, Inc., a tract or tracts of land at or near Guntersville, Alabama;

(*c*) to transfer any part of the possession and control of the real estate now in possession of and under the control of said Corporation to any other department, agency, or instrumentality of the United States: *Provided, however*, That no land shall be conveyed, leased, or transferred, upon which there is located any permanent dam, hydroelectric power plant, or munitions plant heretofore or hereafter built by or for the United States or for the Authority, except that this prohibition shall not apply to the transfer of Nitrate Plant Numbered 1, at Muscle Shoals, Alabama, or to Waco Quarry: *And provided further*, That no transfer authorized herein in (a) or (c), except leases for terms of less than twenty years, shall be made without the approval of the President of the United States, if the property to be conveyed exceeds $500 in value; and

(*d*) to convey by warranty deed, or otherwise, lands, easements, and rights of way to States, counties, municipalities, school districts, railroad companies, telephone, telegraph, water and power companies, where any such conveyance is necessary in order to replace any such lands, easements, or rights-of-way to be flooded or destroyed as the result of the construction of any dam or reservoir now under construction by the Corporation, or subsequently authorized by Congress, and easements and rights of way upon which are located transmission or distribution lines. The Corporation shall also have power to convey or lease Nitrate Plant Numbered 1, at Muscle Shoals, Alabama, and Waco Quarry, with the approval of the War Department and the President. [49 Stat. 1076, as amended by 55 Stat. 599.]

(l) Shall have power to advise and cooperate in the readjustment of the population displaced by the construction of dams, the acquisition of reservoir areas, the protection of watersheds, the acquisition of rights of way, and other necessary acquisitions of land, in order to effectuate the purposes of the Act; and may cooperate with Federal, State, and local agencies to that end. [49 Stat. 1080.]

Sec. 5. The board is hereby authorized—

(a) To contract with commercial producers for the production of such fertilizers or fertilizer materials as may be needed in the Government's program of development and introduction in excess of that produced by Government plants. Such contracts may provide either for outright purchase of materials by the board or only for the payment of carrying charges on special materials manufactured at the board's request for its program.

(b) To arrange with farmers and farm organizations for large-scale practical use of the new forms of fertilizers under conditions permitting an accurate measure of the economic return they produce. [48 Stat. 61.]

(c) To cooperate with National, State, district, or county experimental stations or demonstration farms, with farmers, landowners, and associations of farmers or landowners, for the use of new forms of fertilizer or fertilizer practices during the initial or experimental period of their introduction, and for promoting the prevention of soil erosion by the use of fertilizers and otherwise. [48 Stat. 61, as amended by 49 Stat. 1076.]

(d) The board in order to improve and cheapen the production of fertilizer is authorized to manufacture and sell fixed nitrogen, fertilizer, and fertilizer ingredients at Muscle Shoals by the employment of existing facilities, by modernizing existing plants, or by any other process or processes that in its judgment shall appear wise and profitable for the fixation of atmospheric nitrogen or the cheapening of the production of fertilizer.

(e) Under the authority of this Act the board may make donations or sales of the product of the plant or plants operated by it to be fairly and equitably distributed through the agency of county demonstration agents, agricultural colleges, or otherwise as the board may direct, for experimentation, education, and introduction of the use of such products in cooperation with practical farmers so as to obtain information as to the value, effect, and best methods of their use.

(f) The board is authorized to make alterations, modifications, or improvements in existing plants and facilities, and to contruct new plants.

(g) In the event it is not used for the fixation of nitrogen for agricultural purposes or leased, then the board shall maintain in stand-by condition nitrate plant numbered 2, or its equivalent, for the fixation of atmospheric nitrogen, for the production of explosives in the event of war or a national emergency, until the Congress shall by joint resolution release the board from this obligation, and if any part thereof be used by the board for the manufacture of phosphoric acid or potash, the balance of nitrate plant numbered 2 shall be kept in stand-by condition.

(h) To establish, maintain, and operate laboratories and experimental plants, and to undertake experiments for the purpose of enabling the Corporation to furnish nitrogen products for military purposes, and nitrogen and other fertilizer products for agricultural purposes in the most economical manner and at the highest standard of efficiency.

(i) To request the assistance and advice of any officer, agent, or employee of any executive department or of any independent office of the United States, to enable the Corporation the better to carry out its power successfully, and as far as practicable shall utilize the services of such officers, agents, and employees, and the President shall, if in his opinion, the public interest, service, or economy so require, direct that such assistance, advice, and service be rendered to the Corporation, and any individual that may be by the President directed to render such assistance, advice, and service shall be thereafter subject to the orders, rules, and regulations of the board: *Provided*, That any invention or discovery made by virtue of and incidental to such service by an employee of the Government of the United States serving under this section, or by any employee of the Corporation, together with any patents which may be granted thereon, shall be the sole and exclusive property of the Corporation, which is hereby authorized to grant such licenses thereunder as shall be authorized by the board: *Provided further*, That the board may pay to such inventor such sum from the income from sale of license as it may deem proper.

(j) Upon the requisition of the Secretary of War* or the Secretary of the Navy to manufacture for and sell at cost to the United States explosives or their nitrogenous content.

(k) Upon the requisition of the Secretary of War the Corporation shall allot and deliver without charge to the War Department so much power as shall be necessary in the judgment of said Department for use in operation of all locks, lifts, or other facilities in aid of navigation.

(l) To produce, distribute, and sell electric power, as herein particularly specified.

(m) No products of the Corporation shall be sold for use outside of the United States, its Territories and possessions, except to the United States Government for the use of its Army and Navy, or to its allies in case of war.

(n) The President is authorized, within twelve months after the passage of this Act, to lease to any responsible farm organization or to any corporation organized by it nitrate plant numbered 2 and Waco Quarry, together with the railroad connecting said quarry with nitrate plant numbered 2, for a term not exceeding fifty years at a rental of not less than $1 per year, but such authority shall be subject to the express condition that the lessee shall use said property during the term of said lease exclusively for the manufacture of fertilizer and fertilizer ingredients to be used only in the manufacture of fertilizer by said lessee and sold for use as fertilizer. The said lessee shall convenant to keep said property in first-class condition, but the lessee shall be authorized to modernize said plant numbered 2 by the installation of such machinery as may be necessary, and is authorized to amortize the cost of said machinery and improvements over the term of said lease or any part thereof. Said lease shall also provide that the board shall sell to the lessee power for the operation of said plant at the same schedule of prices that it charges all other customers for power of the same class and quantity. Said lease shall also provide that, if the said lessee does not desire to buy power of the publicly owned plant, it shall have the right to purchase its power for the operation of said plant of the Alabama Power Company or any other publicly or privately owned corporation engaged in the generation and sale of electric power, and in such case the lease shall provide further that the said lessee shall have a free right of way to build a transmission line over Government property to said plant paying the actual expenses and damages, if any, incurred by the Corporation on account of such line. Said lease shall also provide that the said lessee shall covenant that during the term of said lease the said lessee shall not enter into any illegal monopoly, combination, or trust with any privately owned corporation en-

---

* The title of the Secretary of War was changed to Secretary of the Army by section 205 of the Act of July 26, 1947, 61 Stat. 501.

gaged in the manufacture, production, and sale of fertilizer with the object or effect of increasing the price of fertilizer to the farmer. [48 Stat. 61–63.]

SEC. 6. In the appointment of officials and the selection of employees for said Corporation, and in the promotion of any such employees or officials, no political test or qualification shall be permitted or given consideration, but all such appointments and promotions shall be given and made on the basis of merit and efficiency. Any member of said board who is found by the President of the United States to be guilty of a violation of this section shall be removed from office by the President of the United States, and any appointee of said board who is found by the board to be guilty of a violation of this section shall be removed from office by said board. [48 Stat. 63.]

SEC. 7. In order to enable the Corporation to exercise the powers and duties vested in it by this Act—

(a) The exclusive use, possession, and control of the United States nitrate plants numbered 1 and 2, including steam plants, located, respectively, at Sheffield, Alabama, and Muscle Shoals, Alabama, together with all real estate and buildings connected therewith, all tools and machinery, equipment, accessories, and materials belonging thereto, and all laboratories and plants used as auxiliaries thereto; the fixed-nitrogen research laboratory, the Waco limestone quarry, in Alabama, and Dam Numbered 2, located at Muscle Shoals, its power house, and all hydroelectric and operating appurtenances (except the locks), and all machinery, lands, and buildings in connection therewith, and all appurtenances thereof, and all other property to be acquired by the Corporation in its own name or in the name of the United States of America, are hereby entrusted to the Corporation for the purposes of this Act.

(b) The President of the United States is authorized to provide for the transfer to the Corporation of the use, possession, and control of such other real or personal property of the United States as he may from time to time deem necessary and proper for the purposes of the Corporation as herein stated. [48 Stat. 63.]

SEC. 8. (a) The Corporation shall maintain its principal office in the immediate vicinity of Muscle Shoals, Alabama. The Corporation shall be held to be an inhabitant and resident of the northern judicial district of Alabama within the meaning of the laws of the United States relating to the venue of civil suits.

(b) The Corporation shall at all times maintain complete and accurate books of accounts.

(c) Each member of the board, before entering upon the duties of his office, shall subscribe to an oath (or affirmation) to support the Constitution of the United States and to faithfully and impartially perform the duties imposed upon him by this Act. [48 Stat. 63.]

SEC. 9. (a) The board shall file with the President and with the Congress, in December of each year, a financial statement and a complete report as to the business of the Corporation covering the preceding governmental fiscal year. This report shall include an itemized statement of the cost of power at each power station, the total number of employees and the names, salaries, and duties of those receiving compensation at the rate of more than $1,500 a year. [48 Stat. 63.]

(b) All purchases and contracts for supplies or services, except for personal services, made by the Corporation, shall be made after advertising, in such manner and at such times sufficiently in advance of opening bids, as the board shall determine to be adequate to insure notice and opportunity for competition: *Provided,* That advertisement shall not be required when, (1) an emergency requires immediate delivery of the supplies or performance of the services; or (2) repair parts, accessories, supplemental equipment, or services are required for supplies or services previously furnished or contracted for; or (3) the aggregate amount involved in any purchase of supplies or procurement of services does not exceed $500; in which cases such purchases of supplies or procurement of services may be made in the open market in the manner common among businessmen: *Provided further,* That in comparing bids and in making awards the board may consider such factors as relative quality and adaptability of supplies or services, the bidder's financial responsibility, skill, experience, record of integrity in dealing, ability to furnish repairs and maintenance services, the time of delivery or performance offered, and whether the bidder has complied with the specifications.

The Comptroller General of the United States shall audit the transactions of the Corporation at such times as he shall determine, but not less frequently than once each governmental fiscal year, with personnel of his selection. In such connection he and his representatives shall have free and open access to all papers, books, records, files, accounts, plants, warehouses, offices, and all other things, property, and places belonging to or under the control of or used or employed by the Corporation, and shall be afforded full facilities for counting all cash and verifying transactions with and balances in depositories. He shall make report of each such audit in quadruplicate, one copy for the President of the United States, one for the chairman of the board, one for public inspection at the principal office of the Corporation, and the other to be retained by him for the uses of the Congress: *Provided,* That such report shall not be made until the Corporation shall have had reasonable opportunity to examine the exceptions and criticisms of the Comptroller General or the General Accounting Office, to point out errors therein, explain or answer the same, and to file a statement which shall be submitted by the Comptroller General with his report. The expenses for each such audit shall be paid from any appropriation or appropriations for the General Accounting Office, and such part of such expenses as may be allocated to the cost of generating, transmitting, and distributing electric energy shall be reimbursed promptly by the Corporation as billed by the Comptroller General. The Comptroller General shall make special report to the President of the United States and to the Congress of any transaction or condition found by him to be in conflict with the powers or duties entrusted to the Corporation by law. [48 Stat. 63–64, as amended by 49 Stat. 1080–1081.]

Nothing in this Act shall be construed to relieve the Treasurer or other accountable officers or employees of the Corporation from compliance with the provisions of existing law requiring the rendition of accounts for adjustment and settlement pursuant to section 236, Revised Statutes, as amended by section 305 of the Budget and Accounting Act, 1921 (42 Stat. 24), and accounts for all receipts and disbursements by or for the Corporation shall be rendered accordingly: *Provided*, That, subject only to the provisions of the Tennessee Valley Authority Act of 1933, as amended, the Corporation is authorized to make such expenditures and to enter into such contracts, agreements, and arrangements, upon such terms and conditions and in such manner as it may deem necessary, including the final settlement of all claims and litigation by or against the Corporation; and, notwithstanding the provisions of any other law governing the expenditure of public funds, the General Accounting Office, in the settlement of the accounts of the Treasurer or other accountable officer or employee of the Corporation, shall not disallow credit for, nor withhold funds because of, any expenditure which the board shall determine to have been necessary to carry out the provisions of said Act.

The Corporation shall determine its own system of administrative accounts and the forms and contents of its contracts and other business documents except as otherwise provided in the Tennessee Valley Authority Act of 1933, as amended. [55 Stat. 775.]

SEC. 9a. The board is hereby directed in the operation of any dam or reservoir in its possession and control to regulate the stream flow primarily for the purposes of promoting navigation and controlling floods. So far as may be consistent with such purposes, the board is authorized to provide and operate facilities for the generation of electric energy at any such dam for the use of the Corporation and for the use of the United States or any agency thereof, and the board is further authorized, whenever an opportunity is afforded, to provide and operate facilities for the generation of electric energy in order to avoid the waste of water power, to transmit and market such power as in this act provided, and thereby, so far as may be practicable, to assist in liquidating the cost or aid in the maintenance of the projects of the Authority. [49 Stat. 1076.]

SEC. 10. The board is hereby empowered and authorized to sell the surplus power not used in its operations, and for operation of locks and other works generated by it, to States, counties, municipalities, corporations, partnerships, or individuals, according to the policies hereinafter set forth; and to carry out said authority, the board is authorized to enter into contracts for such sale for a term not exceeding twenty years, and in the sale of such current by the board it shall give preference to States, counties, municipalities, and coopera- tive organizations of citizens or farmers, not organized or doing business for profit, but primarily for the purpose of supplying electricity to its own citizens or members: *Provided*, That all contracts made with private companies or individuals for the sale of power, which power is to be resold for a profit, shall contain a provision authorizing the board to cancel said contract upon five years' notice in writing, if the board needs said power to supply the demands of States, counties, or municipalities. In order to promote and encourage the fullest possible use of electric light and power on farms within reasonable distance of any of its transmission lines the board in its discretion shall have power to construct transmission lines to farms and small villages that are not otherwise supplied with electricity at reasonable rates, and to make such rules and regulations governing such sale and distribution of such electric power as in its judgment may be just and equitable: *Provided further*, That the board is hereby authorized and directed to make studies, experiments, and determi- nations to promote the wider and better use of electric power for agricultural and domestic use, or for small or local industries, and it may cooperate with State governments, or their subdivisions or agencies, with educational or re- search institutions, and with cooperatives or other organizations, in the application of electric power to the fuller and better balanced development of the resources of the region [48 Stat. 64]: *Provided further*, That the board is authorized to include in any contract for the sale of power such terms and conditions, including resale rate schedules, and to provide for such rules and regulations as in its judgment may be necessary or desirable for carrying out the purposes of this Act, and in case the purchaser shall fail to comply with any such terms and conditions, or violate any such rules and regulations, said contract may provide that it shall be voidable at the election of the board: *Provided further*, That in order to supply farms and small villages with electric power directly as contemplated by this section, the board in its discretion shall have power to acquire existing electric facilities used in serving such farms and small villages: *And provided further*, That the terms "States," "counties," and "municipalities" as used in this Act shall be construed to include the public agencies of any of them unless the context requires a different construction. [49 Stat. 1076.]

SEC. 11. It is hereby declared to be the policy of the Government so far as practical to distribute and sell the surplus power generated at Muscle Shoals equitably among the States, counties, and municipalities within transmission distance. This policy is further declared to be that the projects herein provided for shall be considered primarily as for the benefit of the people of the section as a whole and particularly the domestic and rural consumers to whom the power can economically be made available, and accordingly that sale to and use by industry shall be a secondary purpose, to be utilized principally to secure a sufficiently high load factor and revenue returns which will permit domestic and rural use at the lowest possible rates and in such manner as to encourage increased domestic and rural use of electricity. It is further hereby declared to be the policy of the Government to utilize the Muscle Shoals properties so far as may be necessary to improve, increase, and cheapen the production of fertilizer and fertilizer ingredients by carrying out the provisions of this Act. [48 Stat. 64–65.]

SEC. 12. In order to place the board upon a fair basis for making such contracts and for receiving bids for the sale of such power, it is hereby expressly authorized, either from appropriations made by Congress or from funds secured from the sale of such power, or from funds secured by the sale of bonds hereafter provided for, to construct, lease, purchase, or authorize the construction of transmission lines within transmission distance from the place where generated, and to interconnect with other systems. The board is also authorized to lease to any person, persons, or corporation the use of any transmission line owned by the Government and operated by the board, but no such lease shall be made that in any way interferes with the use of such transmission line by the board: *Provided*, That if any State, county, municipality, or other public or cooperative organization of citizens or farmers, not organized or doing business for profit, but primarily for the purpose of supplying electricity to its own citizens or members, or any two or more of such municipalities or organizations, shall construct or agree to construct and maintain a properly designed and built transmission line to the Government reservation upon which is located a Government generating plant, or to a main transmission line owned by the Government or leased by the board and under the control of the board, the board is hereby authorized and directed to contract with such State, county, municipality, or other organization, or two or more of them, for the sale of electricity for a term not exceeding thirty years; and in any such case the board shall give to such State, county, municipality, or other organization ample time to fully comply with any local law now in existence or hereafter enacted providing for the necessary legal authority for such State, county, municipality, or other organization to contract with the board for such power. *Provided further,* That all contracts entered into between the Corporation and any municipality or other political subdivision or cooperative organization shall provide that the electric power shall be sold and distributed to the ultimate consumer without discrimination as between consumers of the same class, and such contract shall be voidable at the election of the board if a discriminatory rate, rebate, or other special concession is made or given to any consumer or user by the municipality or other political subdivision or cooperative organization: *And provided further,* That as to any surplus power not so sold as above provided to States, counties, municipalities, or other said organizations, before the board shall sell the same to any person or corporation engaged in the distribution and resale of electricity for profit, it shall require said person or corporation to agree that any resale of such electric power by said person or corporation shall be made to the ultimate consumer of such electric power at prices that shall not exceed a schedule fixed by the board from time to time as reasonable, just, and fair; and in case of any such sale, if an amount is charged the ultimate consumer which is in excess of the price so deemed to be just, reasonable, and fair by the board, the contract for such sale between the board and such distributor of electricity shall be voidable at the election of the board: *And provided further,* That the board is hereby authorized to enter into contracts with other power systems for the mutual exchange of unused excess power upon suitable terms, for the conservation of stored water, and as an emergency or breakdown relief. [48 Stat. 65–66.]

SEC. 12a. In order (1) to facilitate the disposition of the surplus power of the Corporation according to the policies set forth in this Act; (2) to give effect to the priority herein accorded to States, counties, municipalities, and nonprofit organizations in the purchase of such power by enabling them to acquire facilities for the distribution of such power; and (3) at the same time to preserve existing distribution facilities as going concerns and avoid duplication of such facilities, the board is authorized to advise and cooperate with and assist, by extending credit for a period of not exceeding five years to, States, counties, municipalities and nonprofit organizations situated within transmission distance from any dam where such power is generated by the Corporation in acquiring, improving, and operating (a) existing distribution facilities and incidental works, including generating plants; and (b) interconnecting transmission lines; or in acquiring any interest in such facilities, incidental works, and lines. [49 Stat. 1076–1077.]

SEC. 13. In order to render financial assistance to those States and local governments in which the power operations of the Corporation are carried on and in which the Corporation has acquired properties previously subject to State and local taxation, the board is authorized and directed to pay to said States, and the counties therein, for each fiscal year, beginning July 1, 1940, the following percentages of the gross proceeds derived from the sale of power by the Corporation for the preceding fiscal year as hereinafter provided, together with such additional amounts as may be payable pursuant to the provisions hereinafter set forth, said payments to constitute a charge against the power operations of the Corporation: For the fiscal year (beginning July 1) 1940, 10 per centum; 1941, 9 per centum; 1942, 8 per centum; 1943, $7\frac{1}{2}$ per centum; 1944, 7 per centum; 1945, $6\frac{1}{2}$ per centum; 1946, 6 per centum; 1947, $5\frac{1}{2}$ per centum; 1948 and each fiscal year thereafter, 5 per centum. "Gross proceeds", as used in this section, is defined as the total gross proceeds derived by the Corporation from the sale of power for the preceding fiscal year, excluding power used by the Corporation or sold or delivered to any other department or agency of the Government of the United States for any purpose other than the resale thereof. The payments herein authorized are in lieu of taxation, and the Corporation, its property, franchises and income, are hereby expressly exempted from taxation in any manner or form by any State, county, municipality, or any subdivision or district thereof.

The payment for each fiscal year shall be apportioned among said States in the following manner: One-half of said payment shall be apportioned by paying to each State the percentage thereof which the gross proceeds of the power sales by the Corporation within said State during the preceding fiscal year bears to the total gross proceeds from all power sales by the Corporation during the preceding fiscal year; the remaining one-half of said payment shall be apportioned by paying to each State the percentage thereof which the book value of the power property held by the Corporation within said State at the end of the preceding fiscal year bears to the total book value of all such property held by the Corporation on the same date. The book value of power property shall include that portion of the investment allocated or estimated to be allocable to power: *Provided*, That the minimum annual payment to each State (including payments to counties therein) shall not be less than an amount equal to the two-year average of the State and local ad valorem property taxes levied against power property purchased and operated by the Corporation in said State and against that portion of reservoir lands related to dams constructed by or on behalf of the United States Government and held or operated by the Corporation and allocated or estimated to be allocable to power. The said two-year average shall be calculated for the last two tax years during which said property was privately owned and operated or said land was privately owned: *Provided further*, That the minimum annual payment to each State in which the Corporation owns and operates power property (including payments to counties therein) shall not be less than $10,000 in any case: *Provided further*, That the corporation shall pay directly to the respective counties the two-year average of county ad valorem property taxes (including taxes levied by taxing districts within the respective counties) upon power property and reservoir lands allocable to power, determined as above provided, and all payments to any such county within a State shall be deducted from the payment otherwise due to such State under the provisions of this section. The determination of the board of the amounts due hereunder to the respective States and counties shall be final.

The payments above provided shall in each case be made to the State or county in equal monthly installments beginning not later than July 31, 1940.

Nothing herein shall be construed to limit the authority of the Corporation in its contracts for the sale of power to municipalities, to permit or provide for the resale of power at rates which may include an amount to cover tax-equivalent payments to the municipality in lieu of State, county, and municipal taxes upon any distribution system or property owned by the municipality, or any agency thereof, conditioned upon a proper distribution by the municipality of any amounts collected by it in lieu of State or county taxes upon any such distribution system or property; it being the intention of Congress that either the municipality or the State in which the municipality is situated shall provide for the proper distribution to the State and county of any portion of tax equivalent so collected by the municipality in lieu of State or county taxes upon any such distribution system or property.

The Corporation shall, not later than January 1, 1945, submit to the Congress a report on the operation of the provisions of this section, including a statement of the distribution to the various States and counties hereunder; the effect of the operation of the provisions of this section on State and local finances; an appraisal of the benefits of the program of the Corporation to the States and counties receiving payments hereunder, and the effect of such benefits in increasing taxable values within such States and counties; and such other data, information, and recommendations as may be pertinent to future legislation. [48 Stat. 66, as amended by 54 Stat. 626–627.]

Sec. 14. The board shall make a thorough investigation as to the present value of Dam Numbered 2, and the steam plants at nitrate plant numbered 1, and nitrate plant numbered 2, and as to the cost of Cove Creek Dam, for the purpose of ascertaining how much of the value or the cost of said properties shall be allocated and charged up to (1) flood control, (2) navigation, (3) fertilizer, (4) national defense, and (5) the development of power. The findings thus made by the board, when approved by the President of the United States, shall be final, and such findings shall thereafter be used in all allocation of value for the purpose of keeping the book value of said properties. In like manner, the cost and book value of any dams, steam plants, or other similar improvements hereafter constructed and turned over to said board for the purpose of control and management shall be ascertained and allocated. [48 Stat. 66.]

The board shall, on or before January 1, 1937, file with Congress a statement of its allocation of the value of all such properties turned over to said board, and which have been completed prior to the end of the preceding fiscal year, and shall thereafter in its annual report to Congress file a statement of its allocation of the value of such properties as have been completed during the preceding fiscal year.

For the purpose of accumulating data useful to the Congress in the formulation of legislative policy in matters relating to the generation, transmission, and distribution of electric energy and the production of chemicals necessary to national defense and useful in agriculture, and to the Federal Power Commission and other Federal and State agencies, and to the public, the board shall keep complete accounts of its costs of generation, transmission, and distribution of electric energy and shall keep a complete account of the total cost of generating and transmission facilities constructed or otherwise acquired by the Corporation, and of producing such chemicals, and a description of the major components of such costs according to such uniform system of accounting for public utilities as the Federal Power Commission has, and if it have none, then it is hereby empowered and directed to prescribe such uniform system of accounting, together with records of such other physical data and operating statistics of the Authority as may be helpful in determining the actual cost and value of services, and the practices, methods, facilities, equipment, appliances, and standards and sizes, types, location, and geographical and economic integration of plants and systems best suited to promote the public interest, efficiency, and the wider and more economical use of electric energy. Such data shall be reported to the Congress by the board from time to time with appropriate analyses and recommendations, and, so far as practicable, shall be made available to the Federal Power Commission and other Federal and State agencies which may be concerned with the administration of legislation relating to the generation, transmission, or distribution of elecric energy and chemicals useful to agriculture. It is hereby declared to be the policy of this Act that, in order, as soon as practicable, to make the power projects self-supporting and self-liquidating, the surplus power shall be sold at rates which, in the opinion of the board, when applied to the normal capacity of the Authority's power facilities, will produce gross revenues in excess of the cost of production of said power and in addition to the statement of the cost of power at each power station as required by section 9 (a) of the "Tennessee Valley Act of 1933", the board shall file with each annual report, a statement of the total cost of all power generated by it at all power stations during each year, the average cost of such power per kilowatt hour, the rates at which sold, and to whom sold, and copies of all contracts for the sale of power. [49 Stat. 1077.]

SEC. 15. In the construction of any future dam, steam plant, or other facility, to be used in whole or in part for the generation or transmission of electric power the board is hereby authorized and empowered to issue on the credit of United States and to sell serial bonds not exceeding $50,000,000 in amount, having a maturity not more than fifty years from the date of issue thereof, and bearing interest not exceeding $3\frac{1}{2}$ per centum per annum. Said bonds shall be issued and sold in amounts and prices approved by the Secretary of the Treasury, but all such bonds as may be so issued and sold shall have equal rank. None of said bonds shall be sold below par, and no fee, commission, or compensation whatever shall be paid to any person, firm, or corporation for handling, negotiating the sale, or selling the said bonds. All of such bonds so issued and sold shall have all the rights and privileges accorded by law to Panama Canal bonds, authorized by section 8 of the Act of June 28, 1902, chapter 1302, as amended by the Act of December 21, 1905 (ch. 3, sec. 1, 34 Stat. 5), as now compiled in section 743 of title 31 of the United States Code. All funds derived from the sale of such bonds shall be paid over to the Corporation. [48 Stat. 66–67.]

SEC. 15a. With the approval of the Secretary of the Treasury, the Corporation is authorized to issue bonds not to exceed in the aggregate $50,000,000 outstanding at any one time, which bonds may be sold by the Corporation to obtain funds to carry out the provisions of section 12a of this Act. Such bonds shall be in such forms and denominations, shall mature within such periods not more than fifty years from the date of their issue, may be redeemable at the option of the Corporation before maturity in such manner as may be stipulated therein, shall bear such rates of interest not exceeding $3\frac{1}{2}$ per centum per annum, shall be subject to such terms and conditions, shall be issued in such manner and amount, and sold at such prices, as may be prescribed by the Corporation, with the approval of the Secretary of the Treasury: *Provided*, That such bonds shall not be sold at such prices or on such terms as to afford an investment yield to the holders in excess of $3\frac{1}{2}$ per centum per annum. Such bonds shall be fully and unconditionally guaranteed both as to interest and principal by the United States, and such guaranty shall be expressed on the face thereof, and such bonds shall be lawful investments, and may be accepted as security, for all fiduciary, trust, and public funds, the investment or deposit of which shall be under the authority or control of the United States or any officer or officers therof. In the event that the Corporation should not pay upon demand, when due, the principal of, or interest on, such bonds, the Secretary of the Treasury shall pay to the holder the amount thereof, which is hereby authorized to be appropriated out of any moneys in the Treasury not otherwise appropriated, and thereupon to the extent of the amount so paid the Secretary of the Treasury shall succeed to all the rights of the holders of such bonds. The Secretary of the Treasury, in his discretion, is authorized to purchase any bonds issued hereunder, and for such purpose the Secretary of the Treasury is authorized to use as a public-debt transaction the proceeds from the sale of any securities hereafter issued under the Second Liberty Bond Act, as amended, and the purposes for which securities may be issued under such Act, as amended, are extended to include any purchases of the Corporation's bonds hereunder. The Secretary of the Treasury may, at any time, sell any of the bonds of the Corporation acquired by him under this section. All redemptions, purchases, and sales by the Secretary of the Treasury of the bonds of the Corporation shall be treated as public-debt transactions of the United States. With the approval of the Secretary of the Treasury, the Corporation shall have power to purchase such bonds in the open market at any time and at any price. No bonds shall be issued hereunder to provide funds or bonds necessary for the performance of any proposed contract negotiated by the Corporation under the authority of section 12a of this Act until the proposed contract shall have been submitted to and approved by the Federal Power Commission. When any such proposed contract shall have been submitted to the said Commission, the matter shall be given precedence and shall be in every way expedited and the Commission's determination of the matter shall be final. The authority of the Corporation to issue bonds hereunder shall expire at the end of five years from the date when this section as amended herein becomes law, except that such bonds may be issued at any time after the expiration of said period to provide bonds or funds necessary for the performance of any contract entered into by the Corporation, prior to the expiration of said period, under the authority of section 12a of this Act. [49 Stat. 1078.]

Sec. 15b. No bonds shall be issued by the Corporation after the date of enactment of this section under section 15 or section 15a.

Sec. 15c. With the approval of the Secretary of the Treasury the Corporation is authorized, after the date of enactment of this section, to issue bonds not to exceed in the aggregate $61,500,000. Such bonds may be sold by the Corporation to obtain funds which may be used for the following purposes only:

(1) Not to exceed $46,000,000 may be used for the purchase of electric utility properties of the Tennessee Electric Power Company and Southern Tennessee Power Company as contemplated in the contract between the Corporation and the Commonwealth and Southern Corporation and others, dated as of May 12, 1939.

(2) Not to exceed $6,500,000 may be used for the purchase and rehabilitation of electric utility properties of the Alabama Power Company and Mississippi Power Company in the following named counties in northern Alabama and northern Mississippi: The counties of Jackson, Madison, Limestone, Lauderdale, Colbert, Lawrence, Morgan, Marshall, De Kalb, Cherokee, Cullman, Winston, Franklin, Marion, and Lamar in northern Alabama, and the counties of Calhoun, Chickasaw, Monroe, Clay, Lowndes, Oktibbeha, Choctaw, Webster, Noxubee, Winston, Neshoba, and Kemper in northern Mississippi.

(3) Not to exceed $3,500,000 may be used for rebuilding, replacing, and repairing electric utility properties purchased by the Corporation in accordance with the foregoing provisions of this section.

(4) Not to exceed $3,500,000 may be used for constructing electric transmission lines, substations, and other electrical facilities necessary to connect the electric utility properties purchased by the Corporation in accordance with the foregoing provisions of this section with the electric power system of the Corporation.

(5) Not to exceed $2,000,000 may be used for making loans under section 12a to States, counties, municipalities, and nonprofit organizations to enable them to purchase any electric utility properties referred to in the contract between the Corporation and the Commonwealth and Southern Corporation and others, dated as of May 12, 1939, or any electric utility properties of the Alabama Power Company or Mississippi Power Company in any of the counties in northern Alabama or nothern Mississippi named in paragraph (2).

The Corporation shall file with the President and with the Congress in December of each year a financial statement and complete report as to the expenditure of funds derived from the sale of bonds under this section covering the period not covered by any such previous statement or report. Such bonds shall be in such forms and denominations, shall mature within such periods not more than fifty years from the date of their issue, may be redeemable at the option of the Corporation before maturity in such manner as may be stipulated therein, shall bear such rates of interest not exceeding $3\frac{1}{2}$ per centum per annum, shall be subject to such terms and conditions, shall be issued in such manner and amount, and sold at such prices, as may be prescribed by the Corporation with the approval of the Secretary of the Treasury:

Provided, That such bonds shall not be sold at such prices or on such terms as to afford an investment yield to the holders in excess of $3\frac{1}{2}$ per centum per annum. Such bonds shall be fully and unconditionally guaranteed both as to interest and principal by the United States, and such guaranty shall be expressed on the face thereof, and such bonds shall be lawful investments, and may be accepted as security, for all fiduciary, trust, and public funds, the investment or deposit of which shall be under the authority or control of the United States or any officer or officers thereof. In the event that the Corporation should not pay upon demand when due, the principal of, or interest on, such bonds, the Secretary of the Treasury shall pay to the holder the amount thereof, which is hereby authorized to be appropriated out of any moneys in the Treasury not otherwise appropriated, and thereupon to the extent of the amount so paid the Secretary of the Treasury shall succeed to all the rights of the holders of such bonds. The Secretary of the Treasury, in his discretion, is authorized to purchase any bonds issued hereunder, and for such purpose the Secretary of the Treasury is authorized to use as a public-debt transaction the proceeds from the sale of any securities hereafter issued under the Second Liberty Bond Act, as amended, and the purposes for which securities may be issued under such Act, as amended, are extended to include any purchases of the Corporation's bonds hereunder. The Secretary of the Treasury may, at any time, sell any of the bonds of the Corporation acquired by him under this section. All redemptions, purchases, and sales by the Secretary of the Treasury of the bonds of the Corporation shall be treated as public-debt transactions of the United States. With the approval of the Secretary of the Treasury, the Corporation shall have power to purchase such bonds in the open market at any time and at any price. None of the proceeds of the bonds shall be used for the performance of any proposed contract negotiated by the Corporation under the authority of section 12a of this Act until the proposed contract shall have been submitted to and approved by the Federal Power Commission. When any such proposed contract shall have been submitted to the said Commission, the matter shall be given precedence and shall be in every way expedited and the Commission's determination of the matter shall be final. The authority of the Corporation to issue bonds under this section shall expire January 1, 1941, except that if at the time such authority expires the amount of bonds issued by the Corporation under this section is less than $61,500,000, the Corporation may, subject to the foregoing provisions of this section, issue, after the expiration of such period, bonds in an amount not in excess of the amount by which the bonds so issued prior to the expiration of such period is less than $61,500,000 for refunding purposes, or, subject to the provisions of paragraph (5) of this section (limiting the purposes for which loans under section 12a of funds derived from bond proceeds may be made) to provide funds found necessary in the performance of any contract entered into by the Corporation prior to the expiration of such period, under the authority of section 12a. [53 Stat. 1083–1085.]

SEC. 16. The board, whenever the President deems it advisable, is hereby empowered and directed to complete Dam Numbered 2 at Muscle Shoals, Alabama, and the steam plant at nitrate plant numbered 2, in the vicinity of Muscle Shoals, by installing in Dam Numbered 2 the additional power units according to the plans and specifications of said dam, and the additional power unit in the steam plant at nitrate plant numbered 2. [48 Stat. 67.]

SEC. 17. The Secretary of War, or the Secretary of the Interior, is hereby authorized to construct, either directly or by contract to the lowest responsible bidder, after due advertisement, a dam in and across Clinch River in the State of Tennessee, which has by long custom become known and designated as the Cove Creek Dam, together with a transmission line from Muscle Shoals, according to the latest and most approved designs, including power house and hydroelectric installations and equipment for the generation of power, in order that the waters of the said Clinch River may be impounded and stored above said dam for the purpose of increasing and regulating the flow of the Clinch River and the Tennessee River below, so that the maximum amount of primary power may be developed at Dam Numbered 2 and at any and all other dams below the said Cove Creek Dam: *Provided, however,* That the President is hereby authorized by appropriate order to direct the employment by the Secretary of War, or by the Secretary of the Interior, of such engineer or engineers as he may designate, to perform such duties and obligations as he may deem proper, either in the drawing of plans and specifications for said dam, or to perform any other work in the building or construction of the same. The President may, by such order, place the control of the construction of said dam in the hands of such engineer or engineers taken from private life as he may desire: *And provided further,* That the President is hereby expressly authorized, without regard to the restriction or limitation of any other statute, to select attorneys and assistants for the purpose of making any investigation he may deem proper to ascertain whether, in the control and management of Dam Numbered 2, or any other dam or property owned by the Government in the Tennessee River Basin, or in the authorization of any improvement therein, there has been any undue or unfair advantage given to private persons, partnerships, or corporations, by any officials or employees of the Government, or whether in any such matters the Government has been injured or unjustly deprived of any of its rights. [48 Stat. 67.]

SEC. 18. In order to enable and empower the Secretary of War, the Secretary of the Interior, or the board to carry out the authority hereby conferred, in the most economical and efficient manner, he or it is hereby authorized and empowered in the exercise of the powers of national defense in aid of navigation, and in the control of the flood waters of the Tennessee and Mississippi Rivers, constituting channels of interstate commerce, to exercise the right of eminent domain for all purposes of this Act, and to condemn all lands, easements, rights of way, and other area necessary in order to obtain a site for said Cove Creek Dam, and the flowage rights for the reservoir of water above said dam, and to negotiate and conclude contracts with States, counties, municipalities, and all State agencies and with railroads, railroad corporations, common carriers, and all public utility commissions and any other person, firm, or corporation, for the relocation of railroad tracks, highways, highway bridges, mills, ferries, electric-light plants, and any and all other properties, enterprises, and projects whose removal may be necessary in order to carry out the provisions of this Act. When said Cove Creek Dam, transmission line, and power house shall have been completed, the possession, use, and control thereof shall be intrusted to the Corporation for use and operation in connection with the general Tennessee Valley project, and to promote flood control and navigation in the Tennessee River. [48 Stat. 67–68.]

SEC. 19. The Corporation, as an instrumentality and agency of the Government of the United States for the purpose of executing its constitutional powers, shall have access to the Patent Office of the United States for the purpose of studying, ascertaining, and copying all methods, formulae, and scientific information (not including access to pending applications for patents) necessary to enable the Corporation to use and employ the most efficacious and economical process for the production of fixed nitrogen, or any essential ingredient of fertilizer, or any method of improving and cheapening the production of hydroelectric power, and any owner of a patent whose patent rights may have been thus in any way copied, used, infringed, or employed by the exercise of this authority by the Corporation shall have as the exclusive remedy a cause of action against the Corporation to be instituted and prosecuted on the equity side of the appropriate district court of the United States, for the recovery of reasonable compensation for such infringement. The Commissioner of Patents shall furnish to the Corporation, at its request and without payment of fees, copies of documents on file in his office: *Provided*, That the benefits of this section shall not apply to any art, machine, method of manufacture, or composition of matter, discovered or invented by such employee during the time of his employment or service with the Corporation or with the Government of the United States. [48 Stat. 68.]

SEC. 20. The Government of the United States hereby reserves the right, in case of war or national emergency declared by Congress, to take possession of all or any part of the property described or referred to in this Act for the purpose of manufacturing explosives or for other war purposes; but, if this right is exercised by the Government, it shall pay the reasonable and fair damages that may be suffered by any party whose contract for the purchase of electric power or fixed nitrogen or fertilizer ingredients is hereby violated, after the amount of the damages has been fixed by the United States Court of Claims in proceedings instituted and conducted for that purpose under rules prescribed by the court. [48 Stat. 68.]

Sec. 21. (a) All general penal statutes relating to the larceny, embezzlement, conversion, or to the improper handling, retention, use, or disposal of public moneys or property of the United States, shall apply to the moneys and property of the Corporation and to moneys and properties of the United States entrusted to the Corporation.

(b) Any person who, with intent to defraud the Corporation, or to deceive any director, officer, or employee of the Corporation or any officer or employee of the United States (1) makes any false entry in any book of the Corporation, or (2) makes any false report or statement for the Corporation, shall, upon conviction thereof, be fined not more than $10,000 or imprisoned not more than five years, or both.

(c) Any person who shall receive any compensation, rebate, or reward, or shall enter into any conspiracy, collusion, or agreement, express or implied, with intent to defraud the Corporation or wrongfully and unlawfully to defeat its purposes, shall, on conviction thereof, be fined not more than $5,000 or imprisoned not more than five years, or both. [48 Stat. 68–69.]

Sec. 22. To aid further the proper use, conservation, and development of the natural resources of the Tennessee River drainage basin and of such adjoining territory as may be related to or materially affected by the development consequent to this Act, and to provide for the general welfare of the citizens of said areas, the President is hereby authorized, by such means or methods as he may deem proper within the limits of appropriations made therefor by Congress, to make such surveys of and general plans for said Tennessee basin and adjoining territory as may be useful to the Congress and to the several States in guiding and controlling the extent, sequence, and nature of development that may be equitably and economically advanced through the expenditure of public funds, or through the guidance or control of public authority, all for the general purpose of fostering an orderly and proper physical, economic, and social development of said areas; and the President is further authorized in making said surveys and plans to cooperate with the States affected thereby, or subdivisions or agencies of such States, or with cooperative or other organizations, and to make such studies, experiments, or demonstrations as may be necessary and suitable to that end. [48 Stat. 69.]

SEC. 23. The President shall, from time to time, as the work provided for in the preceding section progresses, recommend to Congress such legislation as he deems proper to carry out the general purposes stated in said section, and for the especial purpose of bringing about in said Tennessee drainage basin and adjoining territory in conformity with said general purposes (1) the maximum amount of flood control; (2) the maximum development of said Tennessee River for navigation purposes; (3) the maximum generation of electric power consistent with flood control and navigation; (4) the proper use of marginal lands; (5) the proper method of reforestation of all lands in said drainage basin suitable for reforestation; and (6) the economic and social well-being of the people living in said river basin. [48 Stat. 69.]

SEC. 24. For the purpose of securing any rights of flowage, or obtaining title to or possession of any property, real or personal, that may be necessary or may become necessary, in the carrying out of any of the provisions of this Act, the President of the United States for a period of three years from the date of the enactment of this Act, is hereby authorized to acquire title in the name of the United States to such rights or such property, and to provide for the payment for same by directing the board to contract to deliver power generated at any of the plants now owned or hereafter owned or constructed by the Government or by said Corporation, such future delivery of power to continue for a period not exceeding thirty years. Likewise, for one year after the enactment of this Act, the President is further authorized to sell or lease any parcel or part of any vacant real estate now owned by the Government in said Tennessee River Basin, to persons, firms, or corporations who shall contract to erect thereon factories or manufacturing establishments, and who shall contract to purchase of said Corporation electric power for the operation of any such factory or manufacturing establishment. No contract shall be made by the President for the sale of any of such real estate as may be necessary for present or future use on the part of the Government for any of the purposes of this Act. Any such contract made by the President of the United States shall be carried out by the board: *Provided*, That no such contract shall be made that will in any way abridge or take away the preference right to purchase power given in this Act to States, counties, municipalities, or farm organizations: *Provided further*, That no lease shall be for a term to exceed fifty years: *Provided further*, That any sale shall be on condition that said land shall be used for industrial purposes only. [48 Stat. 69–70.]

SEC. 25. The Corporation may cause proceedings to be instituted for the acquisition by condemnation of any lands, easements, or rights of way which, in the opinion of the Corporation, are necessary to carry out the provisions of this Act. The proceedings shall be instituted in the United States district court for the district in which the land, easement, right of way, or other interest, or any part thereof, is located, and such court shall have full jurisdiction to divest the complete title to the property sought to be acquired out of all persons or claimants and vest the same in the United States in fee simple, and to enter a decree quieting the title thereto in the United States of America.

Upon the filing of a petition for condemnation and for the purpose of ascertaining the value of the property to be acquired, and assessing the compensation to be paid, the court shall appoint three commissioners who shall be disinterested persons and who shall take and subscribe an oath that they do not own any lands, or interest or easement in any lands, which it may be desirable for the United States to acquire in the furtherance of said project, and such commissioners shall not be selected from the locality wherein the land sought to be condemned lies. Such commissioners shall receive a per diem of not to exceed $15 for their services, together with an additional amount of $5 per day for subsistence for time actually spent in performing their duties as commissioners.

It shall be the duty of such commissioners to examine into the value of the lands sought to be condemned, to conduct hearings and receive evidence, and generally to take such appropriate steps as may be proper for the determination of the value of the said lands sought to be condemned, and for such purpose the commissioners are authorized to administer oaths and subpoena witnesses, which said witnesses shall receive the same fees as are provided for witnesses in the Federal courts. The said commissioners shall thereupon file a report setting forth their conclusions as to the value of the said property sought to be condemned, making a separate award and valuation in the premises with respect to each separate parcel involved. Upon the filing of such award in court the clerk of said court shall give notice of the filing of such award to the parties to said proceeding, in manner and form as directed by the judge of said court.

Either or both parties may file exceptions to the award of said commissioners within twenty days from the date of the filing of said award in court. Exceptions filed to such award shall be heard before three Federal district judges unless the parties, in writing, in person, or by their attorneys, stipulate that the exceptions may be heard before a lesser number of judges. On such hearing such judges shall pass de novo upon the proceedings had before the commissioners, may view the property, and may take additional evidence. Upon such hearings the said judges shall file their own award, fixing therein the value of the property sought to be condemned, regardless of the award previously made by the said commissioners.

At any time within thirty days from the filing of the decision of the district judges upon the hearing on exceptions to the award made by the commissioners, either party may appeal from such decision of the said judges to the circuit court of appeals, and the said circuit court of appeals shall upon the hearing on said appeal dispose of the same upon the record, without regard to the awards or findings theretofore made by the commissioners or the district judges, and such circuit court of appeals shall thereupon fix the value of the said property sought to be condemned.

Upon acceptance of an award by the owner of any property herein provided to be appropriated, and the payment of the money awarded or upon the failure of either party to file exceptions to the award of the commissioners within the time specified, or upon the award of the commissioners, and the payment of the money by the United States pursuant thereto, or the payment of the money awarded into the registry of the court by the Corporation, the title to said property and the right to the possession thereof shall pass to the United States, and the United States shall be entitled to a writ in the same proceeding to dispossess the former owner of said property, and all lessees, agents, and attorneys of such former owner, and to put the United States, by its corporate creature and agent, the Corporation, into possession of said property.

In the event of any property owned in whole or in part by minors, or insane persons, or incompetent persons, or estates of deceased persons, then the legal representatives of such minors, insane persons, incompetent persons, or estates shall have power, by and with the consent and approval of the trial judge in whose court said matter is for determination, to consent to or reject the awards of the commissioners herein provided for, and in the event that there be no legal representatives, or that the legal representatives for such minors, insane persons, or incompetent persons shall fail or decline to act, then such trial judge may, upon motion, appoint a guardian ad litem to act for such minors, insane persons, or incompetent persons, and such guardian ad litem shall act to the full extent and to the same purpose and effect as his ward could act, if competent, and such guardian ad litem shall be deemed to have full power and authority to respond, to conduct, or to maintain any proceeding herein provided for affecting his said ward. [48 Stat. 70–71.]

SEC. 26. Commencing July 1, 1936, the proceeds for each fiscal year derived by the board from the sale of power or any other products manufactured by the Corporation, and from any other activities of the Corporation including the disposition of any real or personal property, shall be paid into the Treasury of the United States at the end of each calendar year, save and except such part of such proceeds as in the opinion of the board shall be necessary for the Corporation in the operation of dams and reservoirs, in conducting its business in generating, transmitting, and distributing electric energy and in manufacturing, selling, and distributing fertilizer and fertilizer ingredients. A continuing fund of $1,000,000 is also excepted from the requirements of this section and may be withheld by the board to defray emergency expenses and to insure continuous operation: *Provided*, That nothing in this section shall be construed to prevent the use by the board, after June 30, 1936, of proceeds accruing prior to July 1, 1936, for the payment of obligations lawfully incurred prior to such latter date. [48 Stat. 71, as amended by 49 Stat. 1079.]*

SEC. 26a. The unified development and regulation of the Tennessee River system requires that no dam, appurtenant works, or other obstruction, affecting navigation, flood control, or public lands or reservations shall be constructed, and thereafter operated or maintained across, along, or in the said river or any of its tributaries until plans for such construction, operation, and maintenance shall have been submitted to and approved by the board; and the construction, commencement of construction, operation, or maintenance of such structures without such approval is hereby prohibited. When such plans shall have been approved, deviation therefrom either before or after completion of such structures is prohibited unless the modification of such plans has previously been submitted to and approved by the board.

In the event the board shall, within sixty days after their formal submission to the board, fail to approve any plans or modifications, as the case may be, for construction, operation, or maintenance of any such structures on the Little Tennessee River, the above requirements shall be deemed satisfied, if upon application to the Secretary of War, with due notice to the Corporation, and hearing thereon, such plans or modifications are approved by the said Secretary of War as reasonably adequate and effective for the unified development and regulation of the Tennessee River system.

Such construction, commencement of construction, operation, or maintenance of any structures or parts thereof in violation of the provisions of this section may be prevented, and the removal or discontinuation thereof required by the injunction or order of any district court exercising jurisdiction in any district in which such structures or parts thereof may be situated, and the Corporation is hereby authorized to bring appropriate proceedings to this end.

The requirements of this section shall not be construed to be a substitute

* See, as supplementary to this section, the provisions relating to TVA included in Title II of the Government Corporations Appropriation Act, 1948, reprinted *infra* at page 191.

for the requirements of any other law of the United States or of any State, now in effect or hereafter enacted, but shall be in addition thereto, so that any approval, license, permit, or other sanction now or hereafter required by the provisions of any such law for the construction, operation, or maintenance of any structures whatever, except such as may be constructed, operated, or maintained by the Corporation, shall be required, notwithstanding the provisions of this section. [49 Stat. 1079.]

SEC. 27. All appropriations necessary to carry out the provisions of this Act are hereby authorized. [48 Stat. 71.]

SEC. 28. That all Acts or parts of Acts in conflict herewith are hereby repealed, so far as they affect the operations contemplated by this Act. [48 Stat. 71.]

SEC. 29. The right to alter, amend, or repeal this Act is hereby expressly declared and reserved, but no such amendment or repeal shall operate to impair the obligation of any contract made by said Corporation under any power conferred by this Act. [48 Stat. 72.]

SEC. 30. That the sections of this Act are hereby declared to be separable, and in the event of any one or more sections of this Act, or parts thereof, be held to be unconstitutional, such holding shall not affect the validity of other sections or parts of this Act. [48 Stat. 72, as amended by 49 Stat. 1081.]

SEC. 31. This Act shall be liberally construed to carry out the purposes of Congress to provide for the disposition of and make needful rules and regulations respecting Government properties entrusted to the Authority, provide for the national defense, improve navigation, control destructive floods, and promote interstate commerce and the general welfare, but no real estate shall be held except what is necessary in the opinion of the board to carry out plans and projects actually decided upon requiring the use of such land: *Provided*, That any land purchased by the Authority and not necessary to carry out plans and projects actually decided upon shall be sold by the Authority as agent of the United States, after due advertisement, at public auction to the highest bidder, or at private sale as provided in section 4 (k) of this Act. [49 Stat. 1080.]

[PUBLIC—No. 301—77TH CONGRESS, 1ST SESSION*]

[H.R. 3112]

November 21, 1941, 55 Stat. 773

AN ACT

To provide for the alteration, reconstruction, or relocation of certain highway and railroad bridges by the Tennessee Valley Authority

Be it enacted by the Senate and House of Representatives of the United States of America in Congress assembled, That:

Whenever, as the result of the construction of any dam, reservoir, or other improvement under the provisions of the Tennessee Valley Authority Act, or amendments thereto, any bridge, trestle, or other highway or railroad structure located over, upon, or across the Tennessee River or any of its navigable tributaries, including approaches, fenders, and appurtenances thereto, is endangered or otherwise adversely affected and damaged, including any interference with or impairment of its use, to the extent that protection, alteration, reconstruction, relocation, or replacement is necessary or proper to preserve its safety or utility or to meet the requirements of navigation or flood control, or both, the owner or owners of such bridge, trestle, or structure shall be compensated by the Tennessee Valley Authority in the sum of the reasonable actual cost of such protection, alteration, reconstruction, relocation, or replacement: *Provided,* That in arriving at the amount of such compensation the bridge owner shall be charged with a sum which shall equal the net value to the owner of any direct and special benefits accruing to the owner from any improvement or addition or betterment of the altered, reconstructed, relocated, or replaced bridge, trestle, or structure. The Tennessee Valley Authority is empowered to contract with such owner with respect to any such protection, alteration, reconstruction, relocation, or replacement, the payment of the cost thereof and its proper division, which contract may provide either for money compensation or for the performance of all or any part of the work by the Tennessee Valley Authority: *Provided further,* That the payments herein provided for shall be paid out of the earnings of the Authority.

In the event of a failure to agree upon the terms and conditions of any such contract, or upon any default in the performance of any contract entered into

* This statute, while not technically a part of the TVA Act, has such a close connection with the program that it is included here for convenience.

pursuant to this Act, the bridge owner or the Tennessee Valley Authority shall have the right to bring suit to enforce its rights or for a declaration of its rights under this Act, or under any such contract, in the district court of the United States for the district in which the property in question is located. In any such proceeding the court shall apportion the total cost of the work between the Tennessee Valley Authority and the owner in accord with the provisions contained in this section. Any judgment, award, or decree rendered against the Tennessee Valley Authority under this section may be satisfied out of appropriations available for the major project which requires the protection, alteration, reconstruction, relocation, or replacement: *Provided*, That, prior to such alteration, reconstruction, or relocation of said bridges, the location and plans shall be submitted to and approved by the Chief of Engineers and by the Secretary of War in accordance with existing laws.

[PUBLIC—NO. 268—80TH CONGRESS, 1ST SESSION]

[H.R. 3756]

July 30, 1947, 61 Stat. 574, 576–577*

AN ACT

Making appropriations for Government corporations and independent executive agencies for the fiscal year ending June 30, 1948, and for other purposes

Be it enacted by the Senate and the House of Representatives of the United States of America in Congress assembled,

* * * * * * *

TITLE II

* * * * * * *

Not later than June 30, 1948, and not later than June 30 of each calendar year thereafter, until a total of $348,239,240 has been paid as herein provided, the board of directors of the Tennessee Valley Authority shall pay from net income derived the immediately preceding fiscal year from power operations (such net income to be determined by deducting power operating expenses, allocated common expense, and interest on funded debt from total power operating revenues) not less than $2,500,000 of its outstanding bonded indebtedness to the Treasury of the United States exclusive of interest, and such a portion of the remainder of such net income into the Treasury of the United States as miscellaneous receipts as will, in the ten-year period ending June 30, 1958, and in each succeeding ten-year period until the aforesaid total of $348,239,240 shall have been paid, equal not less than a total of $87,059,810, including payment of bonded indebtedness exclusive of interest on such bonded indebtedness. Total payments of not less than $10,500,000 shall be made not later than June 30, 1948.

Amounts equal to the total of all appropriations herein and hereafter made to the Tennessee Valley Authority for power facilities shall be paid by the board of directors thereof, in addition to the total of $348,239,240 specified in the foregoing paragraph, to the Treasury of the United States as miscellaneous receipts, such payments to be amortized over a period of not to exceed forty years after the year in which such facilities go into operation.

None of the power revenues of the Tennessee Valley Authority shall be used for the construction of new power producing projects (except for replacement purposes) unless and until approved by Act of Congress.

* These statutory provisions, while included in an appropriation act, are permanent legislation applicable to TVA, and are accordingly included herein for convenience.

Suggestions for Further Reading

TVA: A Regional Federal Corporation Created in May, 1933 . . .

CASE, H. L. *Personnel Policy in a Public Agency: The TVA Experience.* New York: Harper & Bros., 1955.

This is a book about the development and present status of personnel administration in TVA by its director of personnel. It provides a statement of the principal ideas which have characterized personnel policy and practice in TVA.

DODD, T. I. "Teamwork Approach to Productivity," *Personnel Administration*, XV (January, 1952), 1.

Description of the planning, organization, and functioning of the cooperative union-management committees in TVA, including the operation of the suggestion system.

DURISCH, L. L., and LOWRY, R. E. "Scope and Content of Administrative Decision—the TVA Illustration," *Public Administration Review*, XIII (Autumn, 1953), 219–26.

This paper discusses twelve of the administrative choices made by TVA over a twenty-year period which may be considered the "key decisions" of the agency.

GUNTHER, JOHN. *The Story of TVA.* New York: Harper & Bros., 1951. Pp. 32.

Illustrated with many pictures, this booklet is a description of the TVA operations based upon the material from his book *Inside U.S.A.*

KOHLER, E. L. "TVA and Its Power-Accounting Problems," *Accounting Review*, XXIII (January, 1948), 44–62.

Basic presentation of TVA's accounting system.

KULL, D. C. *Budget Administration in the Tennessee Valley Authority.* ("College of Business Administration, Bureau of Research Study," No. 15.) Knoxville, Tenn.: Division of University Extension for the Bureau of Research, College of Business Administration, and the Bureau of Public Administration, University of Tennessee, 1948. Pp. 64.

Study of TVA's decentralized budget process, which is characterized by its high degree of flexibility.

LILIENTHAL, D. E. *TVA: Democracy on the March.* 20th Anniversary Edition. New York and London: Harper & Bros., 1953. Pp. 294.

This is a new edition of the book first published in 1943. The author, who was then chairman, wrote out of his own experience about this valley because he believed it to represent "a demonstration of the vitality of democracy." New sections have been added, including a chapter on the impact of TVA abroad.

PRITCHETT, C. H. *The Tennessee Valley Authority: A Study in Public Administration*, chap. i, pp. 3–30. Chapel Hill, N.C.: University of North Carolina Press, 1943.

Major emphasis in this book is placed upon the administrative organization and achievements of TVA. The author discusses the background of TVA, its multiple-purpose program, and its historical development. A basic reference liberally footnoted to a wide variety of source material.

RANSMEIER, J. S. *The Tennessee Valley Authority: A Case Study in the Economics of Multiple Purpose Stream Planning*, chaps. i–iii, pp. 3–101. Nashville, Tenn.: Vanderbilt University Press, 1942.

This book first seeks to set out the nature and objectives of TVA by reviewing the facts of its program and by analyzing the philosophy which governs its decisions. Second, it attempts, in a separate part, an analysis of joint-cost apportionment. The author has presented a good summary of historical developments from 1824 to 1932 in the first part of this volume.

TENNESSEE. GOVERNOR [CLEMENT]. *A Report to the President of the United States on the Tennessee Valley Authority, October 8, 1953.* Nashville, Tenn., 1953. Pp. 15.

Governor Clement's statement to the President dealt with the economic development of the Tennessee Valley as a result of TVA. Particular emphasis was placed on the co-operation which exists between TVA and the state and local governments.

TENNESSEE VALLEY AUTHORITY. *Annual Report . . . 1953.* Washington, D.C.: Government Printing Office, 1953. Pp. 171.

An abridged edition of this report has been published under the title *TVA: The Use of the Earth for the Good of Man.*

TENNESSEE VALLEY AUTHORITY. *Facts about TVA Operations.* Knoxville, Tenn.: TVA, 1954. Pp. 20.

This booklet provides answers to most of the questions commonly asked about TVA.

TENNESSEE VALLEY AUTHORITY. *The Norris Project.* ("Technical Report," No. 1.) Washington, D.C.: Government Printing Office, 1940. Pp. 840.

The first of a series of technical reports issued for each project as completed.

TENNESSEE VALLEY AUTHORITY. *Report to the Congress on the Unified Development of the Tennessee River System.* Knoxville, Tenn.: TVA, 1936. Pp. 105.

Recommendations of the board of directors to Congress as to planning, general operating policies to be pursued, and a description of specific recommended projects.

Tennessee Valley Authority Act, May 18, 1933, with Amendments. Washington, D.C.: Government Printing Office, 1942. Pp. 41.

UNITED STATES CONGRESS, HOUSE. COMMITTEE ON PUBLIC WORKS, SUBCOMMITTEE TO STUDY CIVIL WORKS. *Study of Civil Works,* Part III: *Federal Power Commission, Department of Interior, Tennessee Valley Authority . . . Hearings.* . . . 83d Cong., 2d sess. Washington, D.C.: Government Printing Office, 1952. Pp. 693.

Statement by the chairman of the TVA board of directors relating to progress in the Tennessee Valley, 1933–53 (pp. 613–82).

UNITED STATES CONGRESS, SENATE. JOINT COMMITTEE ON LABOR-MANAGEMENT RELATIONS. *Labor-Management Relations in TVA.* (Senate Report 372.) Washington, D.C.: Government Printing Office, 1949. Pp. 63.

This report was prepared by Alexander K. Christie, consultant on labor relations to the Joint Committee. He reviews relations between labor and management under the TVA and Tennessee Valley Trades and Labor Council's general agreement.

To Improve the Navigability and Provide for Flood Control . . .

BARKER, C. T. "Developments in Tennessee River Navigation," *Waterways,* XVII (July, 1953), 13–16; *ibid.,* August, 1953, pp. 31–34.

TVA has issued a twelve-page booklet based on these articles entitled *River Traffic and Industrial Growth.*

BLEE, C. E. "Development of the Tennessee River Waterway," *American Society of Civil Engineers, Centennial Transactions, 1953*, pp. 1132–46.

Tennessee River History is the title of the booklet issued by TVA based on this paper.

CLAPP, G. R. "Experience of the Tennessee Valley Authority in the Comprehensive Development of a River Basin," *United Nations Scientific Conference on the Conservation and Utilization of Resources, Proceedings, Lake Success, New York, August 17–September 6, 1949*, I, 369–75. Lake Success, N.Y., 1950.

FLY, J. L. "Role of the Federal Government in the Conservation and Utilization of Water Resources," *Pennsylvania Law Review*, LXXXVI (January, 1938), 274–94.

Historical outline of waterways developments and multiple-purpose installations undertaken by the government. The author was general counsel for TVA at the time the article was written.

RUTTER, E. J. "Flood-Control Operation of Tennessee Valley Authority Reservoirs," *American Society of Civil Engineers, Transactions*, CXVI (1951), 671–703.

Describes the actual flood conditions in 1946, 1947, and 1948.

TENNESSEE VALLEY AUTHORITY. *TVA Flood Control: A New Concept of Water Control*. Knoxville, Tenn., [1953]. Pp. 12.

TENNESSEE VALLEY AUTHORITY. *Value of Flood Height Reduction from Tennessee Valley Authority Reservoirs to the Alluvial Valley of the Lower Mississippi River*. (House Document 455.) Washington, D.C.: Government Printing Office, 1939. Pp. 64.

To Provide for Reforestation and the Proper Use of Marginal Lands . . .

ARTMAN, J. O. "Forest Development in the Tennessee Valley," *Unasylva*, V (October–December, 1951), 147–53.

Purpose and current activities of the forestry phase of TVA's resource development program are discussed by a staff forester, Division of Forestry Relations of TVA. Illustrations and tables are included.

BAKER, W. M. *TVA Approach to Forest Development*. ("Duke University, School of Forestry Lectures," No. 6.) Durham, N.C.: Duke University, School of Forestry, June, 1946. Pp. 15.

KILBOURNE, RICHARD. "Forestry in the Tennessee Valley," *Yale Forest School News*, XLII (April, 1954), 23–25.

SEIGWORTH, K. J. "Reforestation in the Tennessee Valley," *Public Adminis-tration Review*, VIII (Autumn, 1948), 280–85.

Description of concept of and progress in the reforestation job in the Valley involving about one million acres of eroded, abandoned, or abused land.

TENNESSEE VALLEY AUTHORITY, DIVISION OF FORESTRY RELATIONS. *Fish and Wildlife in the Tennessee Valley*. Norris, Tenn.: TVA, 1950. Pp. 17.

Latest estimates show over two million man-days of fishing each year, and their popularity keeps increasing. Still the waters are not fished to capacity, although there is no closed season.

WIESEHUEGEL, E. G. "Forest Research in the Tennessee Valley," *Southern Lumberman*, CLXXXVI (January 15, 1953), 43–45.

The chief of TVA's Forestry Investigations Branch describes TVA's interests in watershed protection, forest resource development, and utiliza-tion of timber programs.

To Provide for the Agricultural and Industrial Development . . .

CLAPP, G. R. "The Purpose of TVA Fertilizer," *National Fertilizer Review*, XXVII (July–August–September, 1952), 6–7.

This has been reprinted in booklet form by TVA.

ROBOCK, S. H. "Industrialization and Economic Progress in the Southeast," *Southern Economic Journal*, XX (April, 1954), 307–27.

Discussion of some of the problems and opportunities which the region faces as the result of recent economic trends.

TENNESSEE VALLEY AUTHORITY. *Soil . . . People, and Fertilizer Technology*. Washington, D.C.: Government Printing Office, 1949. Pp. 57.

This report deals primarily with TVA's fertilizer production research, including laboratory investigations, pilot-plant operation, and full-scale demonstration-plant production.

TENNESSEE VALLEY AUTHORITY, DEPARTMENT OF AGRICULTURAL RELATIONS. *Food at the Grass Roots: The Nation's Stake in Soil Minerals*. Knoxville, Tenn.: TVA, 1947. Pp. 100.

Data of agronomics, agricultural economics and rural sociology, soil chemistry and chemical engineering, and animal and human nutrition are included in this report by TVA.

TENNESSEE VALLEY AUTHORITY, DIVISION OF CHEMICAL ENGINEERING. *General Outline of Chemical Engineering Activities.* By H. A. CURTIS. Rev. ed. ("Chemical Engineering Report," No. 1.) Washington, D.C.: Government Printing Office, 1949. Pp. 60.

Indicates the basic considerations entering into formulation of the research and fertilizer production program and describes the major projects undertaken. In general, the period covered is from 1933 to 1948.

WENGERT, N. I. *Valley of Tomorrow: The TVA and Agriculture.* ("University of Tennessee Record, Extension Series," Vol. XXVIII, No. 1.) Knoxville, Tenn.: Bureau of Public Administration, University of Tennessee, July, 1952. Pp. 151.

An evaluative study of TVA policies and program administration in the field of agriculture. This analysis reflects the intimate personal experiences and observations of the author as a TVA staff member from 1941 to 1948.

To Provide and Operate Facilities for the Generation of Electric Energy . . .

BLEE, C. E. "Engineering Features of TVA," *American Society of Civil Engineers, Proceedings,* LXXIX, No. 240 (August, 1953), 1–12.

Brief description of the system of dams and reservoirs by TVA's chief engineer.

FOX, A. J., JR. "TVA Dambuilders Turn to Steam," *Engineering News-Record,* CLII (February 25, 1954), 30–34.

Facts and figures on TVA's seven steam plants.

SWIDLER, J. C., and MARQUIS, R. H. "TVA in Court: A Study of TVA's Constitutional Litigation," *Iowa Law Review,* XXXII (January, 1947), 296–326.

TVA's general counsel and his assistant discuss a group of cases which revolved primarily around TVA's electric-power program.

TENNESSEE VALLEY AUTHORITY. *TVA Power—1953.* Knoxville, Tenn.: TVA, 1954. Pp. 25.

This booklet gives, in brief, TVA's objectives, accomplishments, and policies in the field of power.

TENNESSEE VALLEY AUTHORITY. *TVA's Influence on Electric Rates.* Knoxville, Tenn.: TVA, 1954. Pp. 8.

WESSENAUER, G. O. "Power Use in the Tennessee Valley Region," *Tennessee Valley Engineer,* XV (February, 1954), 2–7.

To Aid the Proper Use, Conservation, and Development of the Natural Resources . . .

ACKERMAN, E. A. "Regional Research—Emerging Concepts and Techniques in the Field of Geography," *Economic Geography*, XXIX (July, 1953), 189.

Dr. Ackerman, assistant general manager of TVA, uses TVA as an example of one of the influential forces shaping some regions of the United States.

DURISCH, L. L., and MACON, H. L. *Upon Its Own Resources: Conservation and State Administration*. University, Ala.: University of Alabama Press, 1951. Pp. 136.

This co-operative study is the result of studies done by a group of southern state universities and TVA on the administration of resources in six southeastern states. The authors emphasize the responsibility of the states for natural resource programs and recognize the important influence which the states exert or can exert on both federal and local activities.

KERWIN, J. G. *Federal Water-Power Legislation*. New York: Columbia University Press, 1926. Pp. 396.

The author writes on economic and legal aspects of water power and the various debates in Congress on the struggle between the power companies and conservationists.

MENHINICK, K., and DURISCH, L. L. "Tennessee Valley Authority: Planning in Operation," *Town Planning Review*, XXIV (July, 1953), 116–45.

This paper describes a number of planning activities of TVA and considers the part the agency played in facilitating responsible decision-making in matters relating to regional development. For many years Professor Menhinick was in charge of TVA's regional planning studies; Dr. Durisch is a member of TVA's Government Relations and Economics Staff.

SATTERFIELD, M. H. *Soil and Sky: The Development and Use of Tennessee Valley Resources*. ("University of Tennessee Record, Extension Series," Vol. XXVI, No. 3.) Knoxville, Tenn.: Bureau of Public Administration, University of Tennessee, May, 1950. Pp. 120.

Originally issued by TVA in 1947 under the title *Tennessee Valley Resources: Their Development and Use*. Essentially a progress report on the first fourteen years, stressing the methods and working relationships between TVA and other agencies.

UNITED STATES. PRESIDENT'S WATER RESOURCES POLICY COMMISSION. "The

Tennessee River Basin," *Report of the President's Water Resources Policy Commission*, II, 705–97. Washington, D.C.: Government Printing Office, 1950.

Commissioned by the President to examine into the nation's water resources and determine how they can best be utilized under a fixed policy, this group, in discussing the Tennessee River, traced its development from 1828 to the present TVA program.

And To Promote the General Welfare

BISHOP, E. L. "Health and Safety Services of the Tennessee Valley Authority," *Public Personnel Review*, IV (January, 1943), 9–16.

DERRYBERRY, O. M. "Health Conservation Activities of TVA," *Public Health Reports*, LXVIII (March, 1953), 327–33.

DUFFUS, R. L. *The Valley and Its People*. New York: Alfred A. Knopf, 1946. Pp. 167.

A pictorial story of the nation's first great experiment in rebuilding, by the stimulus of public enterprise, a region laid waste by decades of exploitation. Nearly one hundred photographs give the reader a vivid description of this project.

DURISCH, L. L. "Local Government and the TVA Program," *Public Administration Review*, I (Summer, 1941), 326–34.

How TVA maintains grass-roots contact and co-operates with local governmental agencies.

"Education Helps Build a Region," *High School Journal*, XXIX (May, 1946), 101–71.

This special issue is devoted to resource-use education, describing TVA's approach to the educational program in the Tennessee Valley.

SHAUB, E. L. "TVA: Few Projects in History Ever Did So Much So Quickly for So Many People," *Tennessee Conservationist*, XX (January, 1954), 3–8.

A before-and-after story of how TVA used human ingenuity and the resources of a controlled river to improve the social and economic status of millions of people.

SHELTON, BARRETT. "The Decatur Story," *United Nations Scientific Conference on the Conservation and Utilization of Resources, Proceedings, Lake Success, New York, August 17–September 6, 1949*, I, 376–79. Lake Success, N.Y., 1950.

An account of how one community came from "nothin' to somethin'" in fifteen years of a working partnership between TVA and the people of the town. Also issued as an eleven-page booklet for distribution by TVA.

SOUTH DAKOTA STATE COLLEGE, AGRICULTURAL ECONOMICS DEPARTMENT. *TVA Land Acquisition Experience Applied to Dams in the Missouri Basin.* By KRIS KRISTJANSON. (Bulletin No. 432.) Brookings, S.D., August, 1953. Pp. 47.

An analysis of TVA land acquisition, land management, and family relocation procedures as they could relate to the Missouri Valley development.

TENNESSEE VALLEY AUTHORITY. *Recreation Development of the Tennessee River System.* (House Document 565.) Washington, D.C.: Government Printing Office, 1940. Pp. 99.

"Tennessee Valley Governors Report on TVA," *Congressional Record*, XCIII (April 2, 1947), 3035–37.

Statements obtained from the seven governors in the region affected by TVA, dealing with their relations with TVA's management and the benefits from this program. Published by the *St. Louis Post-Dispatch*, December 31, 1944.

WOLF, BILL. "These Southerners Just Love Yankees," *Saturday Evening Post*, CCXXVI (September 5, 1953), 22–23.

Many benefits in the field of recreation and tourist trade which TVA has brought to the region are described.

Influence Abroad

SEN, SUDHIR. "We Need More River Valley Authorities in India. Part I: TVA Shows the Way," *Indian Journal of Power and River Valley Development*, III (1953), 57–64.

This article shows how TVA's example gives impetus to river planning in India.

TENNESSEE VALLEY AUTHORITY, TECHNICAL LIBRARY. *TVA as a Symbol of Resource Development in Many Countries.* Knoxville, Tenn.: TVA, 1952. Pp. 55.

Brief digest of water-resource developments in a number of countries over the world influenced in some measure by TVA. Bibliographies on each are included.

Additional Bibliographies

TENNESSEE VALLEY AUTHORITY, TECHNICAL LIBRARY. *A Bibliography for the TVA Program.* Knoxville, Tenn.: TVA, July 1, 1953. Pp. 37.

TENNESSEE VALLEY AUTHORITY, TECHNICAL LIBRARY. *Congressional Hearings, Reports, and Documents Relating to TVA, 1933–1952.* Knoxville, Tenn.: TVA, 1954. Pp. 74.

TENNESSEE VALLEY AUTHORITY, TECHNICAL LIBRARY. *An Indexed Bibliography of the Tennessee Valley Authority.* Knoxville, Tenn.: TVA, July, 1936. Pp. 60. (Cumulative supplements are issued each year.)

If the above references are not available, they may be borrowed on inter-library loan from the TVA Technical Library, Knoxville, Tennessee.

Index